BELTER'S HOT
STANDARDS

45 Classics Transposed Down for Women Singers

T0051152

CONTENTS

As Long As He Needs Me

from the Broadway Musical OLIVER!

Words and Music by
LIONEL BART

gone But when he's near me _____ I don't let on _____ The way I

Tempo I

feel in - side _____ The love I have to hide _____ The hell! I've

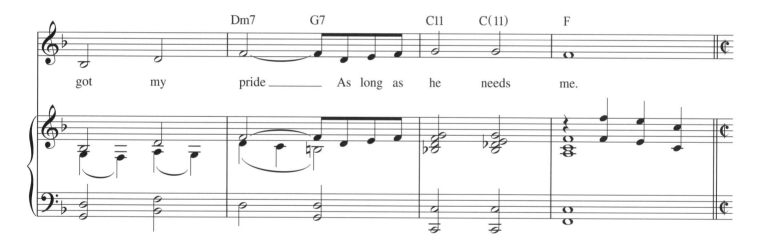

got my pride _____ As long as he needs me.

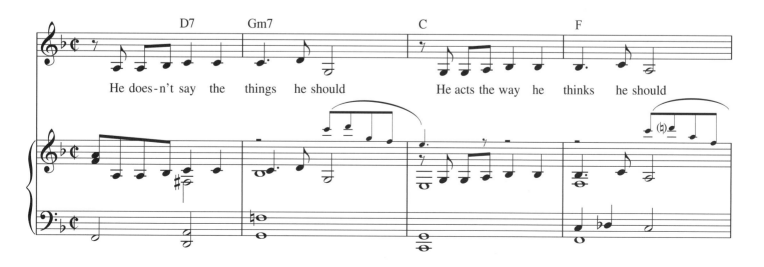

He does-n't say the things he should He acts the way he thinks he should

But all the same I'll play This game his way _____ As long as

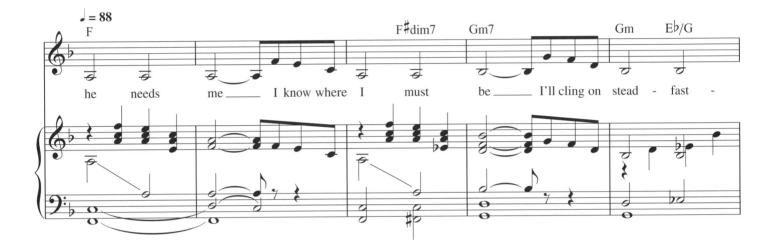

he needs me _____ I know where I must be _____ I'll cling on stead - fast -

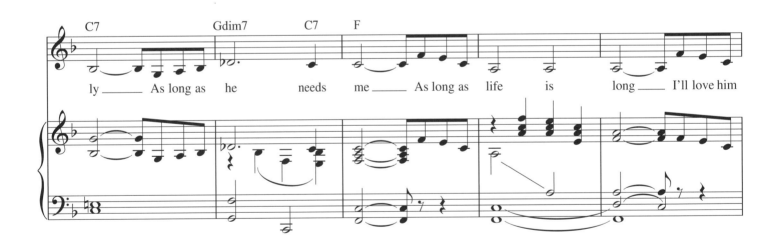

ly _____ As long as he needs me _____ As long as life is long _____ I'll love him

right or wrong _____ And some-how I'll be strong _____ As long as he needs

Black Coffee

Words and Music by PAUL FRANCIS WEBSTER
and SONNY BURKE

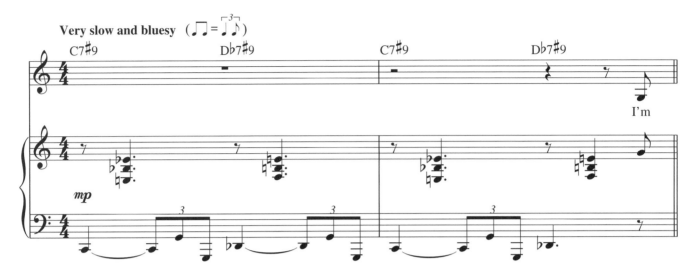

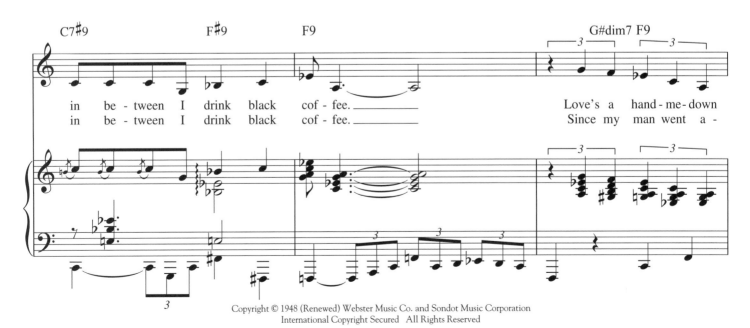

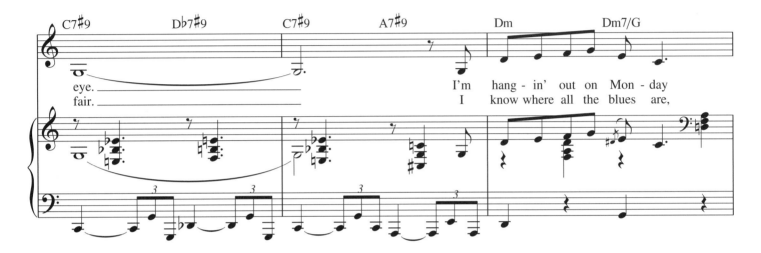

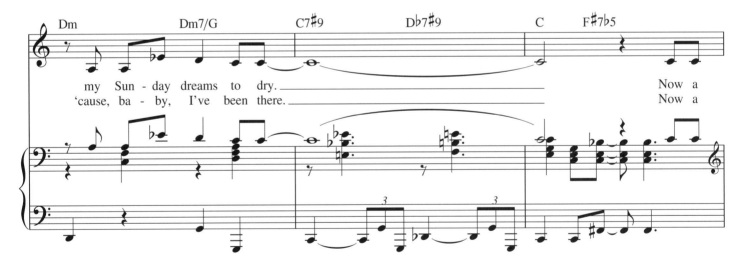

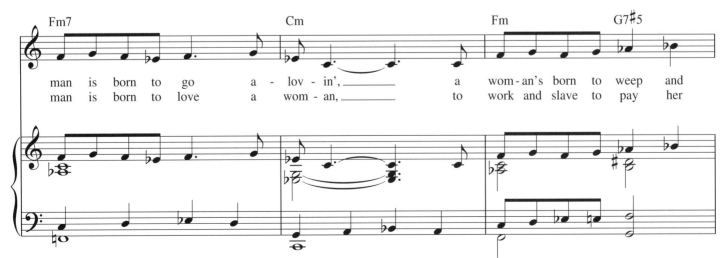

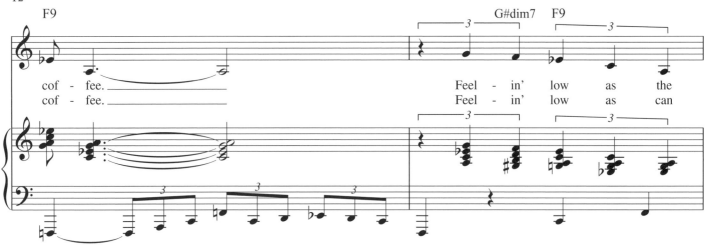

cof - fee. _____ Feel - in' low as the
cof - fee. _____ Feel - in' low as can

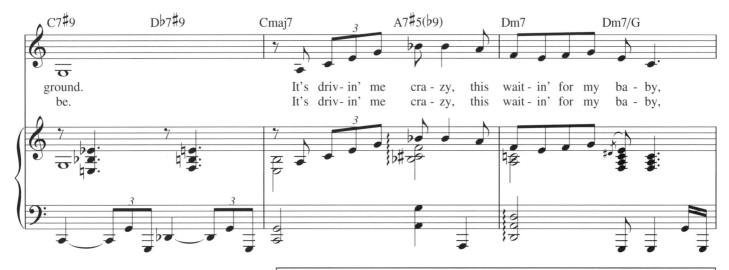

ground. It's driv- in' me cra - zy, this wait- in' for my ba - by,
be. It's driv- in' me cra - zy, this wait- in' for my ba - by,

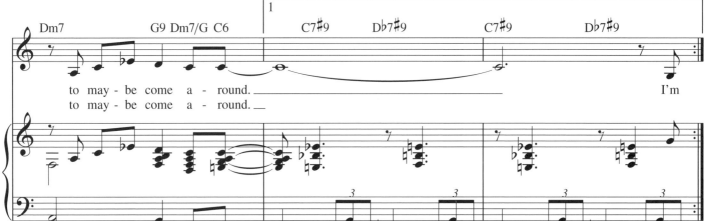

to may- be come a - round. _____ I'm
to may- be come a - round. _____

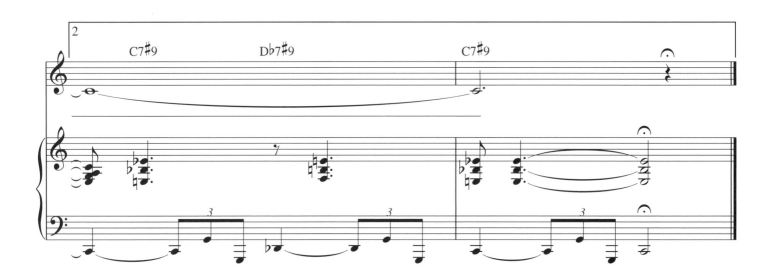

Blue Skies

from BETSY

Words and Music by
IRVING BERLIN

Moderately

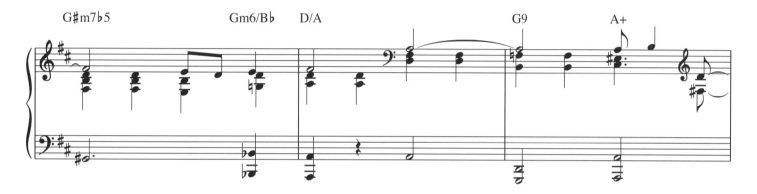

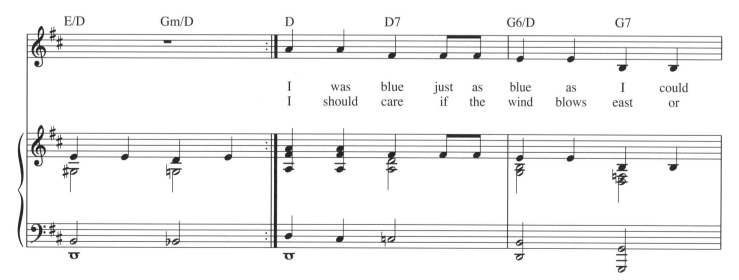

I was blue just as blue as I could
I should care just if the wind blows east or

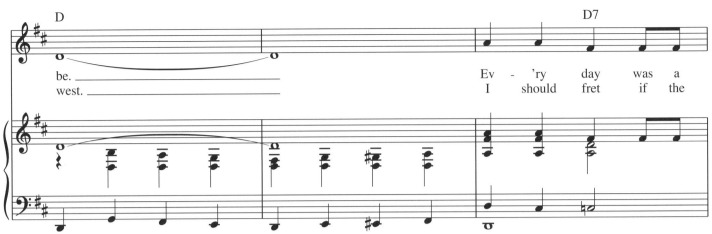

be. _____
west. _____

Ev - 'ry day was a
I should fret if the

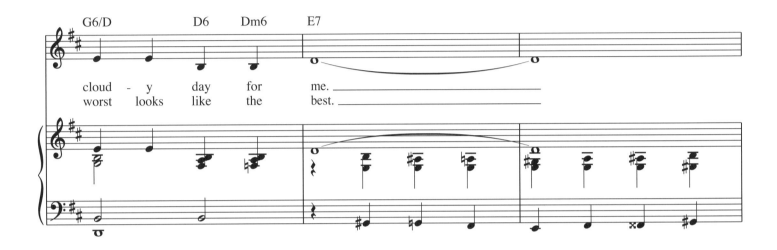

cloud - y day for me. _____
worst looks like the best. _____

Then good luck came a - knock - ing at my door. _____
I should mind if they say it can't be true. _____

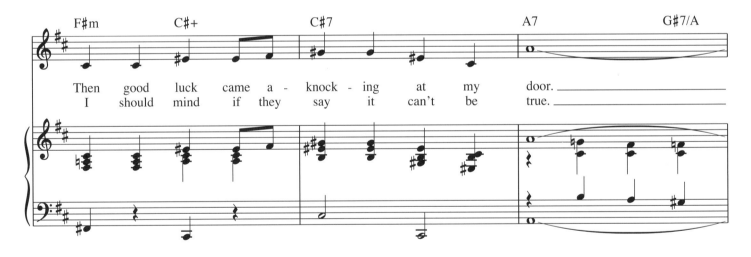

Skies were gray but they're not gray an - y -
I should smile that's ex - act - ly what I

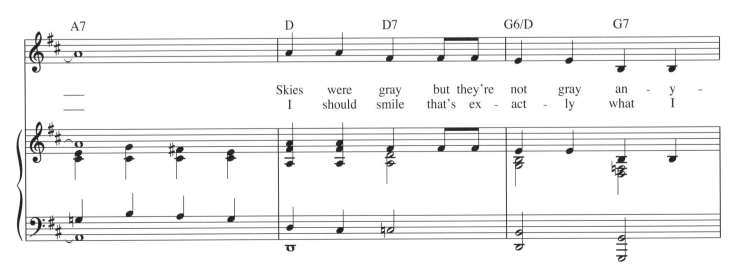

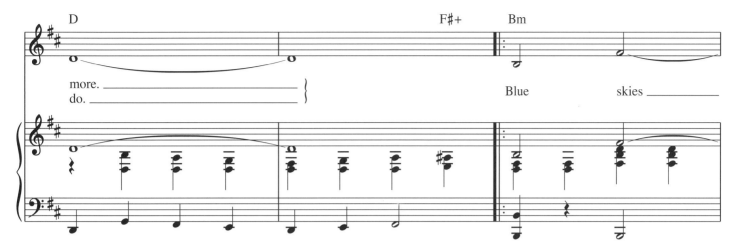

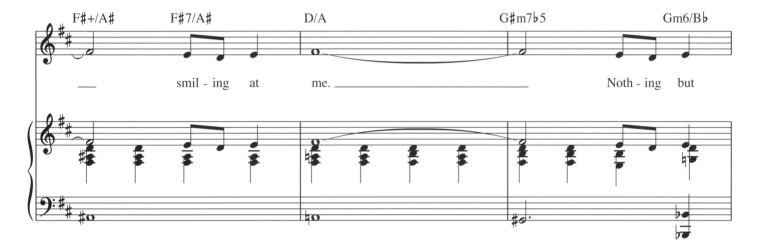

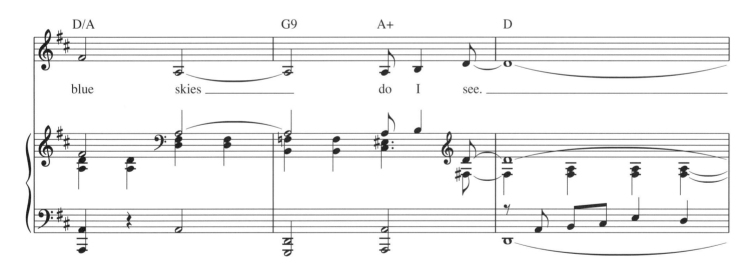

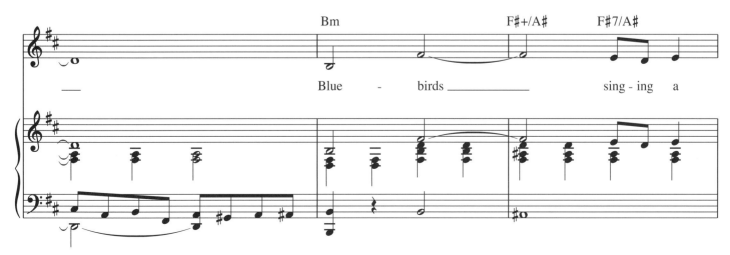

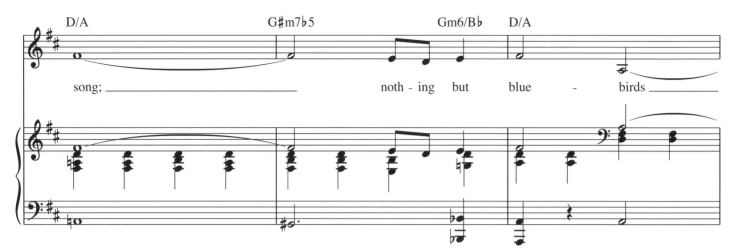

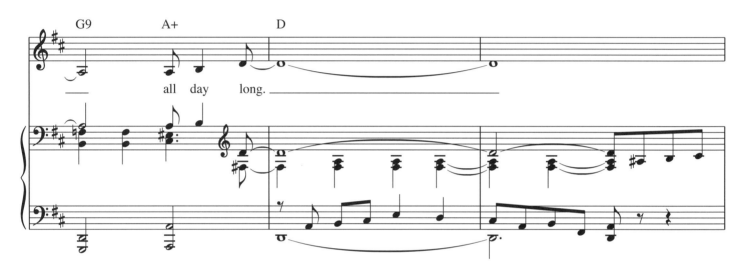

when you're in love, my how they fly. Blue days, _____

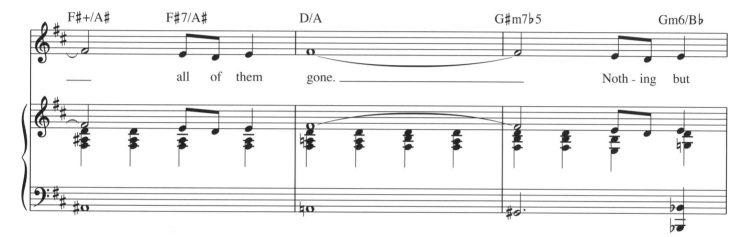

_____ all of them gone. _____ Noth-ing but

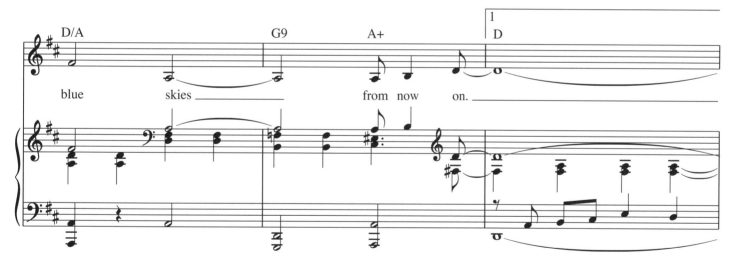

blue skies _____ from now on. _____

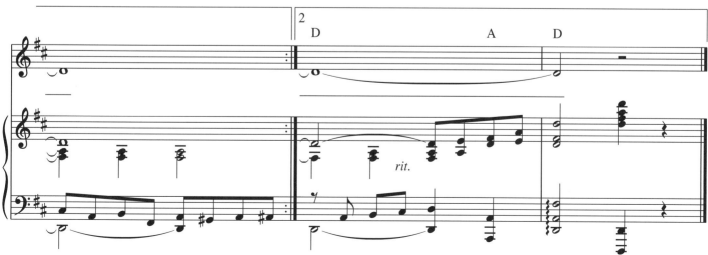

Blame It on My Youth

Words by EDWARD HEYMAN
Music by OSCAR LEVANT

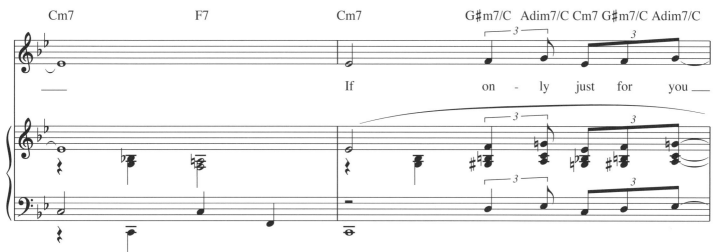

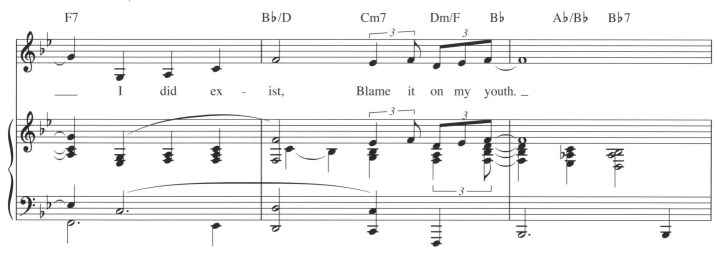

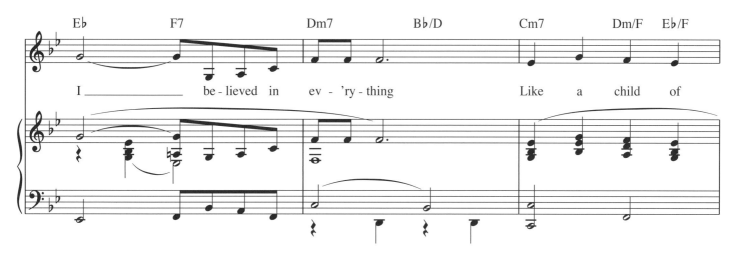

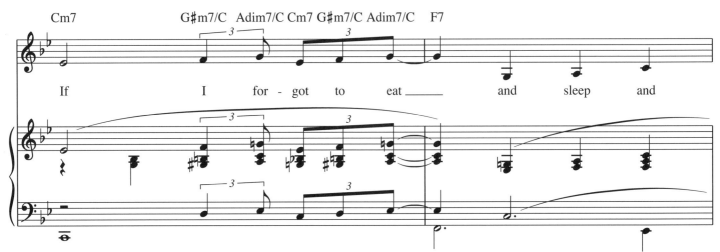

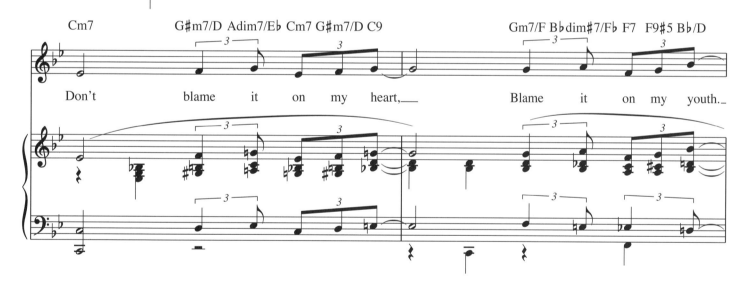

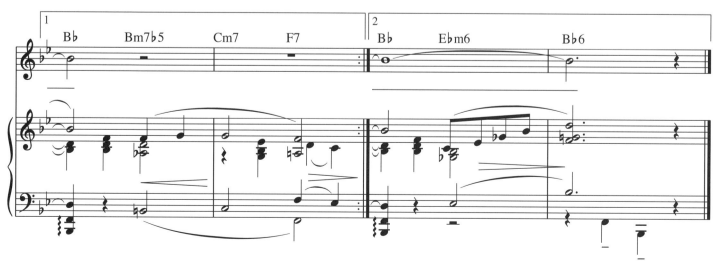

Can't Help Lovin' Dat Man

from SHOW BOAT

Lyrics by OSCAR HAMMERSTEIN II
Music by JEROME KERN

Tempo di Blues *(slowly)*

Oh lis-ten, sis-ter, I love my Mis-ter man _____ and I can't _____ tell yo' why, _____ Dere ain't no rea-son why I should love dat man. _____ It must be sump-in' dat _____

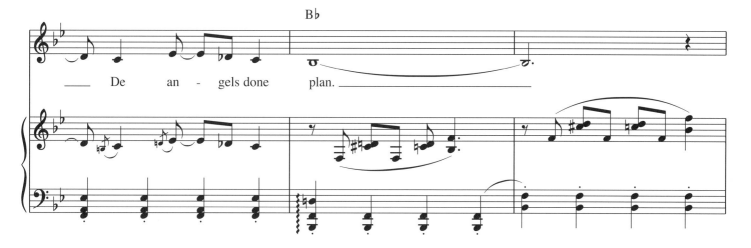

De an - gels done plan. _____

De chimb-ley's smok-in', De roof is leak-in' in, _____ But he don't _

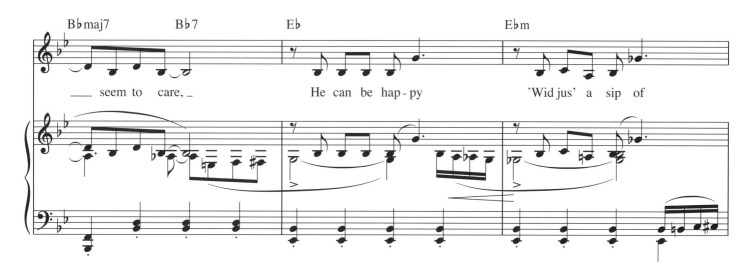

_____ seem to care, _ He can be hap-py 'Wid jus' a sip of

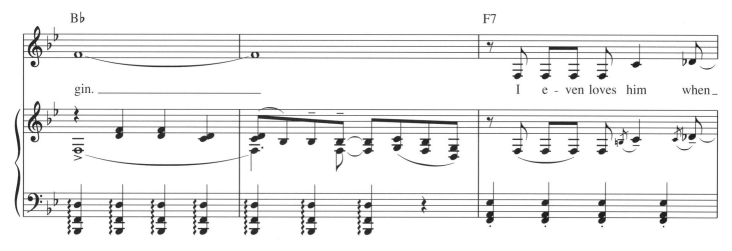

gin. _____ I e-ven loves him when _

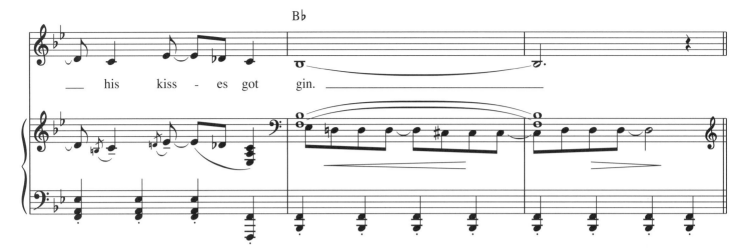

his kiss - es got gin.

Fish got to swim and birds got to fly, I got to love one

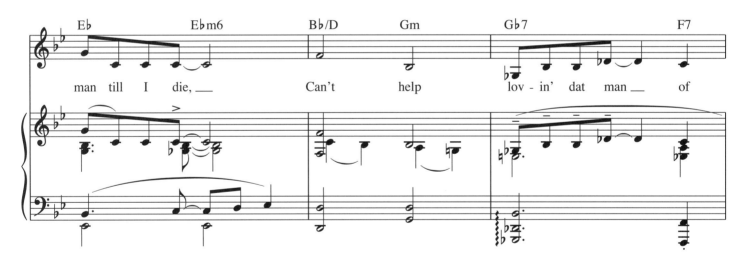

man till I die, Can't help lov - in' dat man of

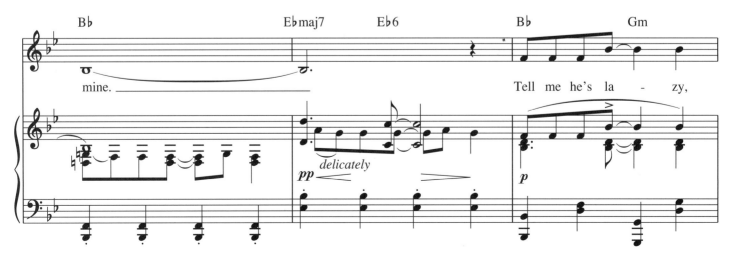

mine. Tell me he's la - zy,

tell me he's slow, _ Tell me I'm cra - zy, may - be, I know, _

Can't help lov - in' dat man _ of mine. _

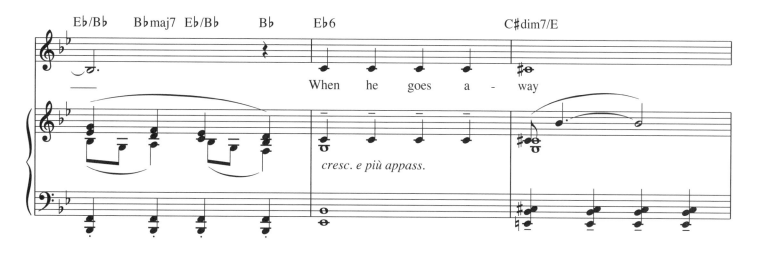

_ When he goes a - way

cresc. e più appass.

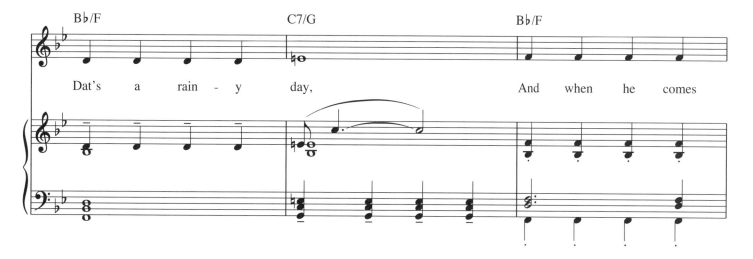

Dat's a rain - y day, And when he comes

back dat day is fine, _____ De sun will shine.

He can come home __ as late as can be, ___ Home wid - out him __ ain't

no home to me, ___ Can't help lov - in' dat man __ of

mine. mine. _____

Don't Get Around Much Anymore

from SOPHISTICATED LADY

Words and Music by DUKE ELLINGTON
and BOB RUSSELL

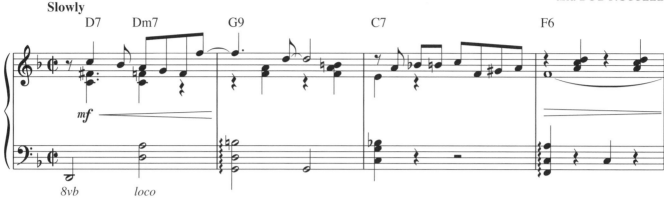

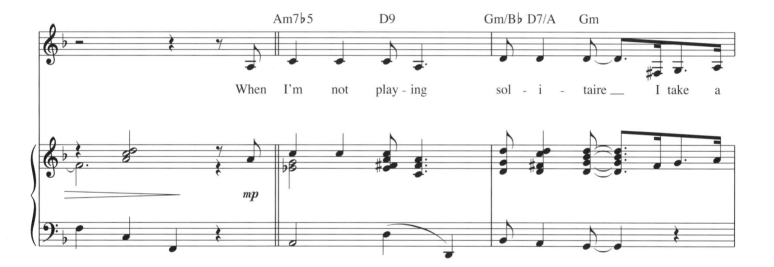

When I'm not play-ing sol - i - taire ___ I take a

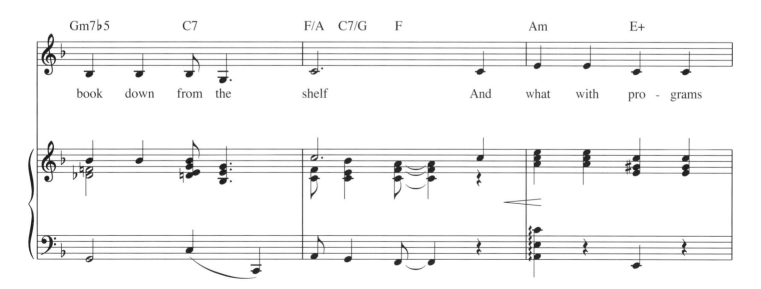

book down from the shelf And what with pro - grams

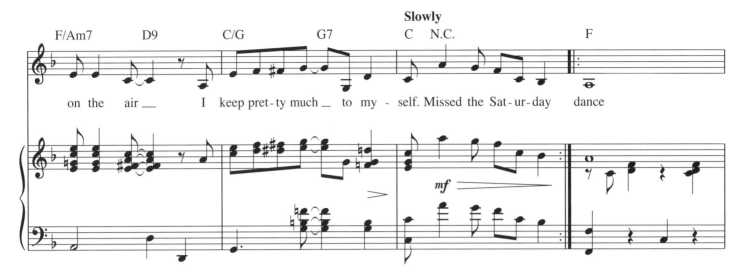

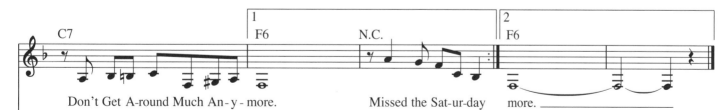

Cry Me a River

Words and Music by
ARTHUR HAMILTON

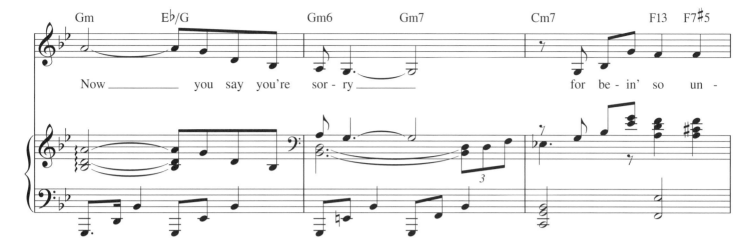

Now you say you're sor - ry for be - in' so un -

true. Well, you can cry me a riv - er, cry me a riv - er,

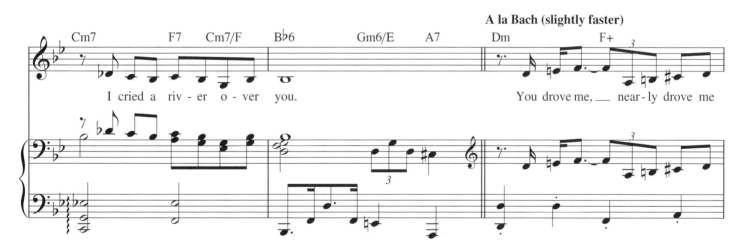

I cried a riv - er o - ver you. You drove me, nearly drove me

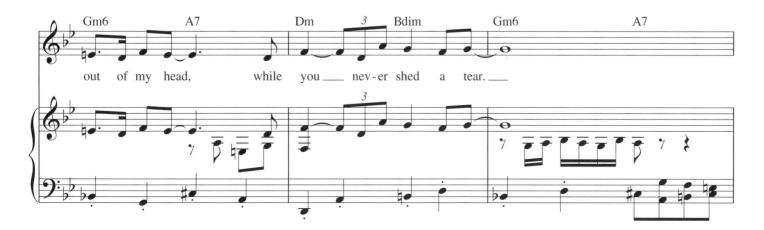

out of my head, while you nev - er shed a tear.

Re - mem - ber? __ I re - mem - ber all that you said; __ told me love was too ple - be - ian,

told me you were thru with me an' now __ you say you love me. __

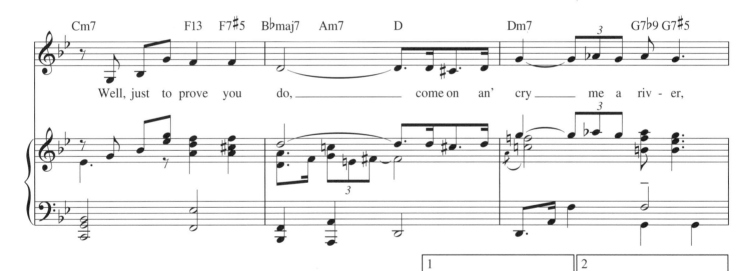

Well, just to prove you do, __ come on an' cry __ me a riv - er,

cry __ me a riv - er, __ I cried a riv - er o - ver you. __ you.

The Glory of Love

from GUESS WHO'S COMING TO DINNER

Words and Music by
BILLY HILL

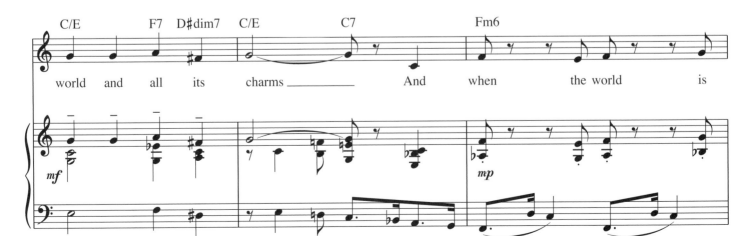

through with us   We've got each oth - ers' arms _____ You've got to

win   a   lit - tle,   lose   a   lit - tle   And al - ways have   the

blues   a lit - tle   That's the sto - ry of,   That's the glo - ry of

love. _____   You've got to   love. _____

God Bless' the Child

Words and Music by ARTHUR HERZOG JR.
and BILLIE HOLIDAY

Slowly, with feeling

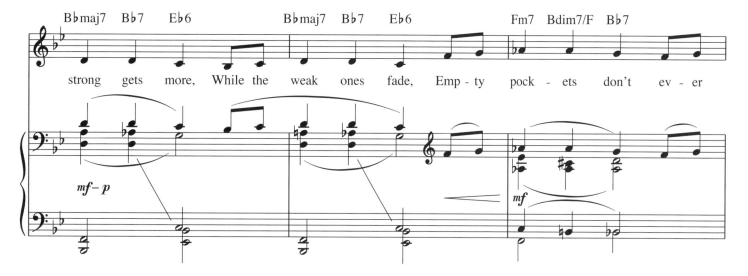

strong gets more, While the weak ones fade, Emp - ty pock - ets don't ev - er

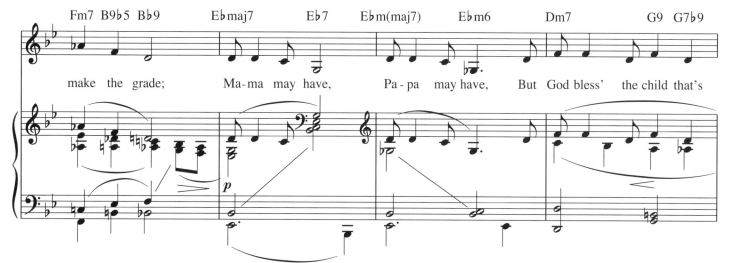

make the grade; Ma-ma may have, Pa-pa may have, But God bless' the child that's

got his own! That's got his own. Mon - ey, you got

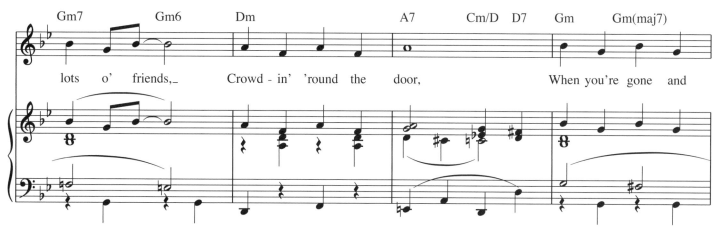

lots o' friends,_ Crowd - in' 'round the door, When you're gone and

A Good Man Is Hard to Find

Words and Music by
EDDIE GREEN

hap - pi - ness, it nev - er lasts a day;　My　heart is al - most break-ing while I
tried my best to treat him nice and kind,　But　now these words are run - ning through my

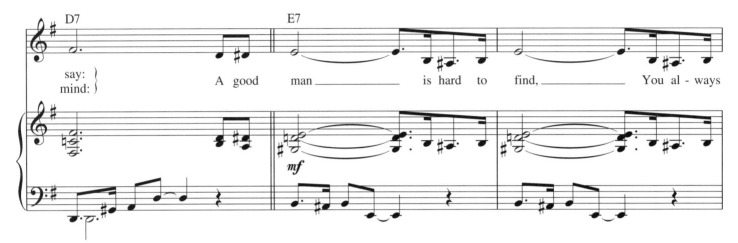

say: ⎫
mind: ⎭　A good man _____ is hard to find, _____ You al - ways

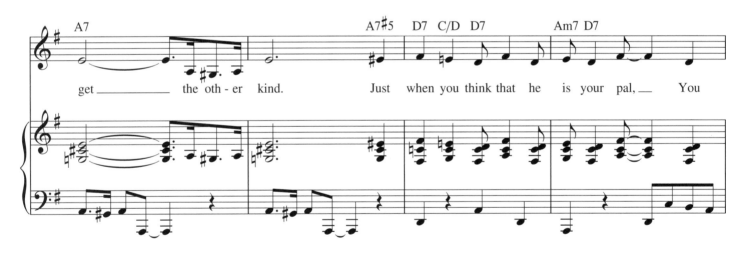

get _____ the oth - er kind.　Just when you think that he is your pal, __ You

look for him and find him fool - ing 'round some oth - er gal. Then you rave; _____ you e - ven

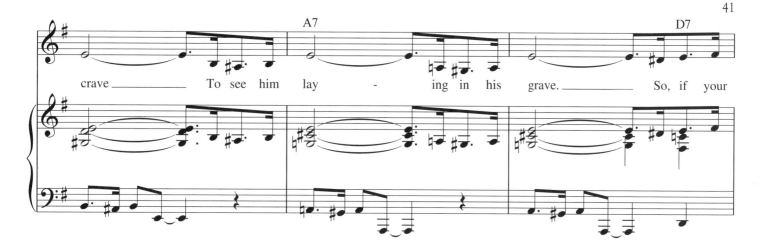

crave _____ To see him lay - ing in his grave. _____ So, if your

man is nice, take my ad - vice __ And hug him in the morn - ing, Kiss him ev -'ry night, __

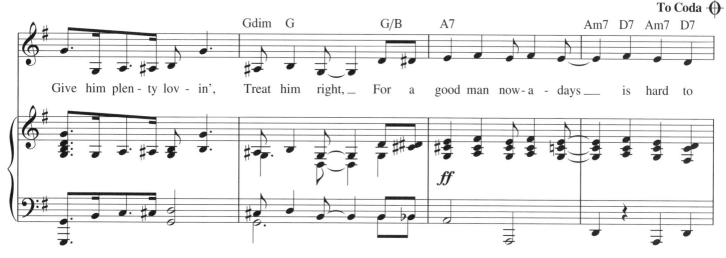

Give him plen - ty lov - in', Treat him right, __ For a good man now-a - days __ is hard to

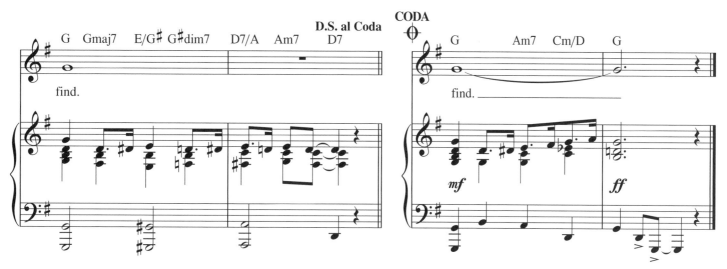

find.

find. _____

He Touched Me

from DRAT! THE CAT!

Lyric by IRA LEVIN
Music by MILTON SCHAFER

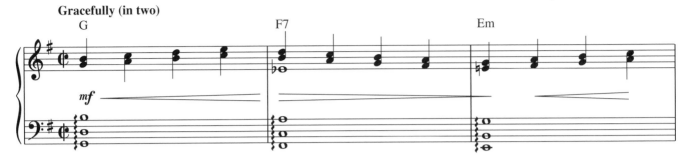

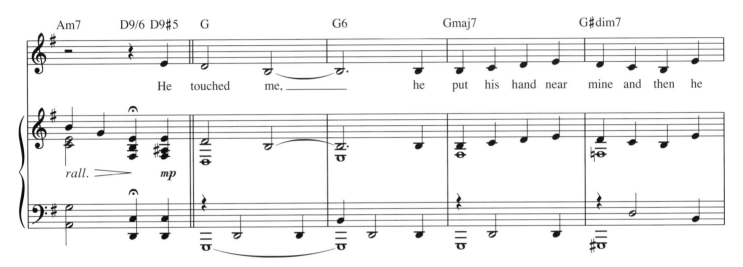

He touched me, _____ he put his hand near mine and then he
touched me, _____

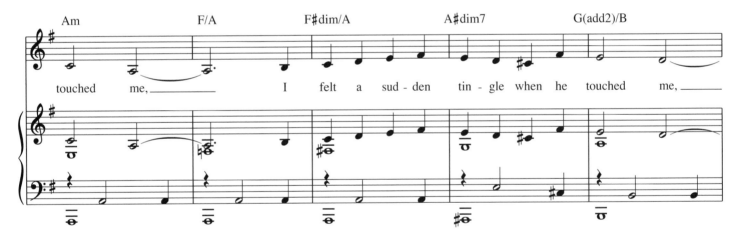

I felt a sud-den tin-gle when he touched me, _____

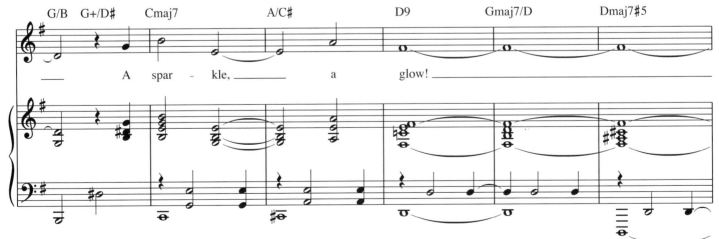

A spar - kle, _____ a glow! _____

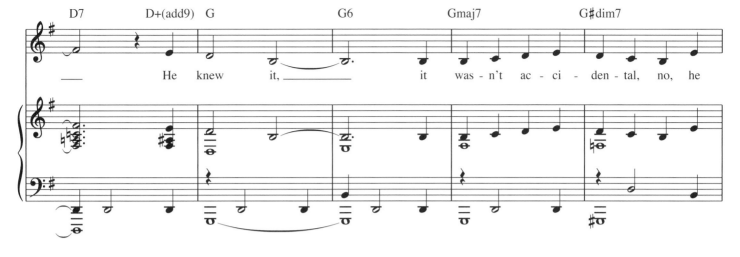

He knew it, _____ _____ it was-n't ac-ci-den-tal, no, he

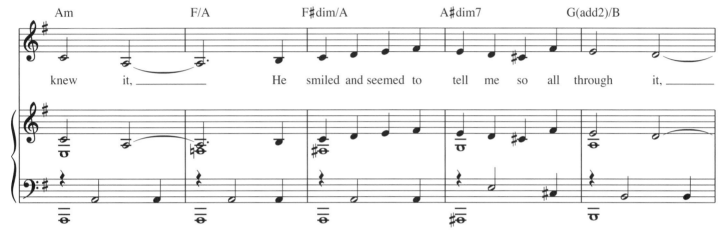

knew it, _____ He smiled and seemed to tell me so all through it, _____

_____ he knew it, _____ I know. _____

_____ He's real _____ and the world is a-live and

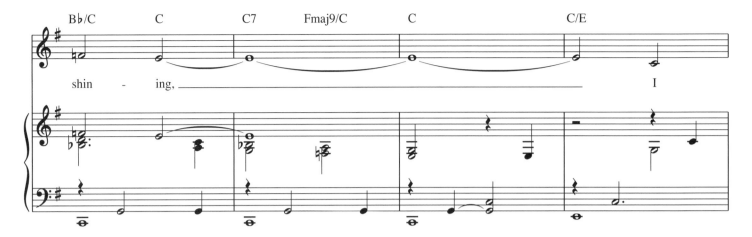

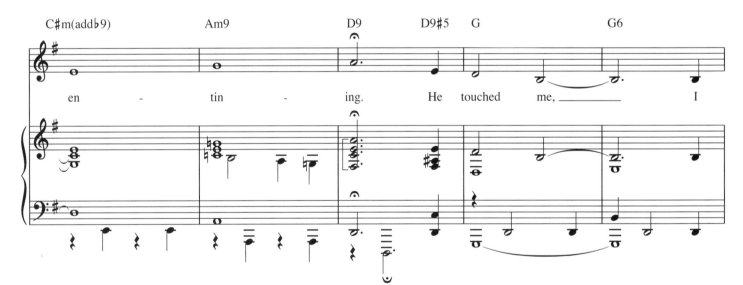

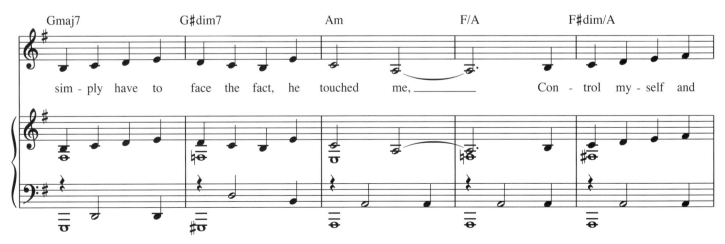

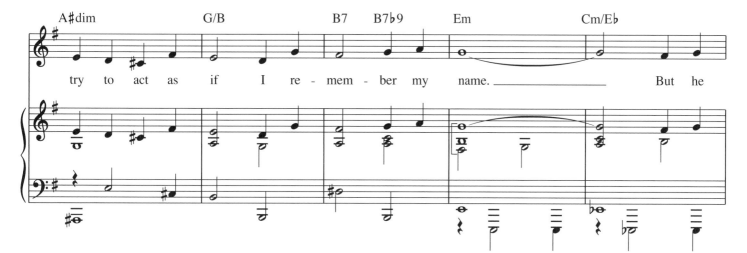

try to act as if I re-mem-ber my name._____ But he

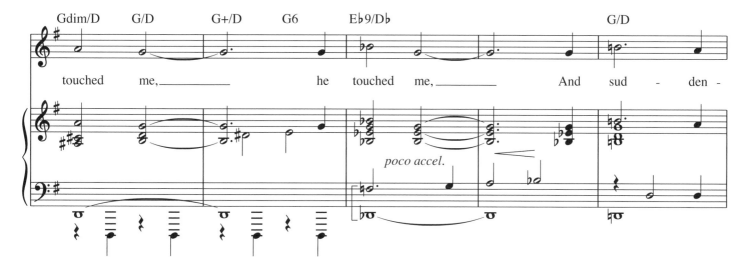

touched me,_____ he touched me,_____ And sud - den-

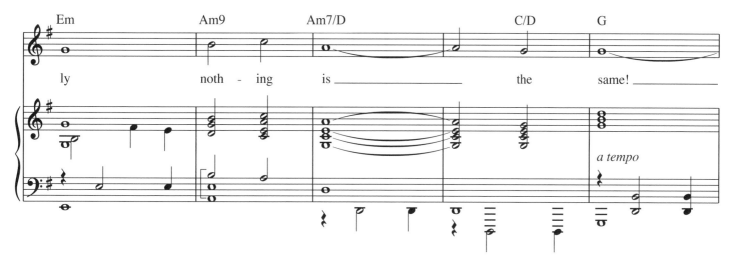

ly noth - ing is _____ the same!_____

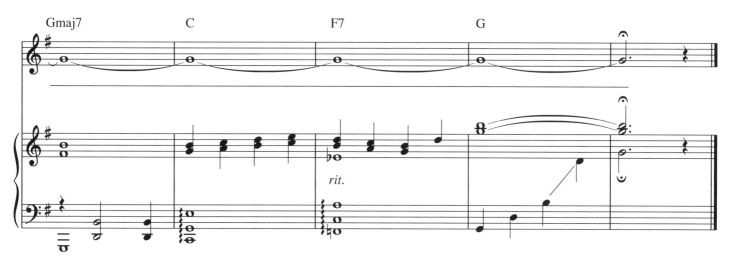

Hit Me With a Hot Note

from SOPHISTICATED LADIES

Words and Music by DUKE ELLINGTON
and DON GEORGE

This standard can be done various ways. This arrangement is based on the version performed in Sophisticated Ladies.

_____ me with a hot note and watch _ me bounce. _ When trum-pets heat _ up,

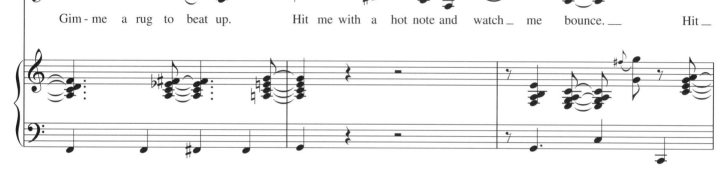

Gim-me a rug to beat up. Hit me with a hot note and watch _ me bounce. _ Hit _

_____ me with a hot note and watch _ me burn, _ Slap _ me down the rhy-thm from stem _

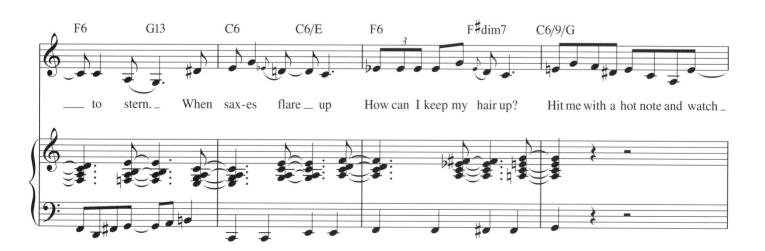

_ to stern. _ When sax-es flare _ up How can I keep my hair up? Hit me with a hot note and watch _

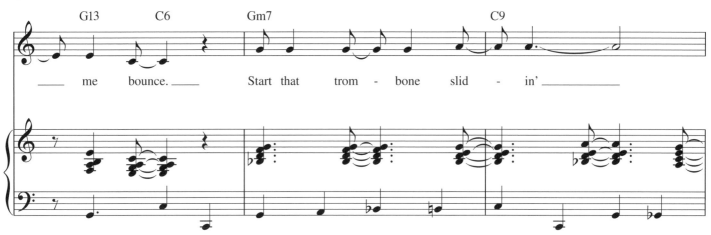

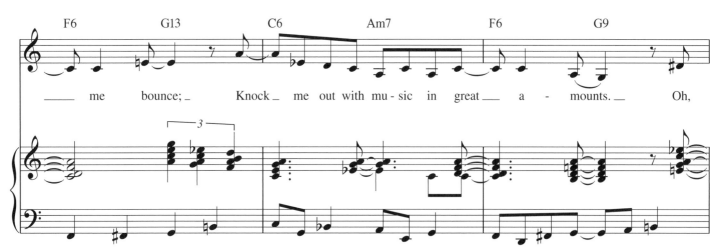

let that beat__ wave, We're gon-na have a heat wave. Hit me with a hot note and watch__

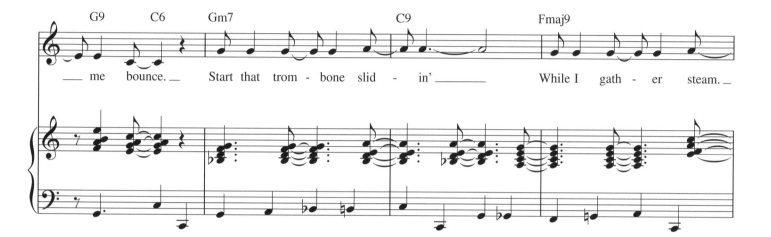

__ me bounce.__ Start that trom-bone slid - in'_____ While I gath - er steam.__

__ Keep that tem - po rid - in',_____

rid - in',_____ keep it rid - in'.__

I Got Lost In His Arms

from ANNIE GET YOUR GUN

Words and Music by
IRVING BERLIN

Moderato

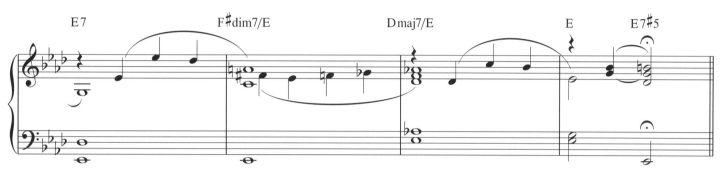

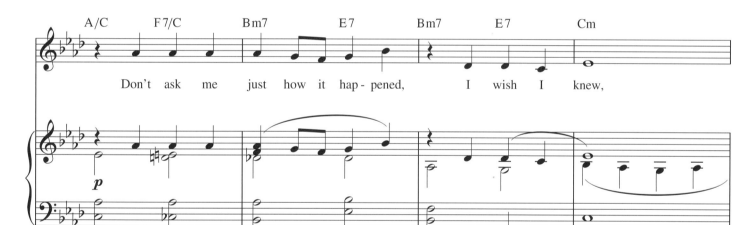

Don't ask me just how it hap-pened, I wish I knew,

I can't be-lieve that it hap-pened, and still it's true. I got

Con anima

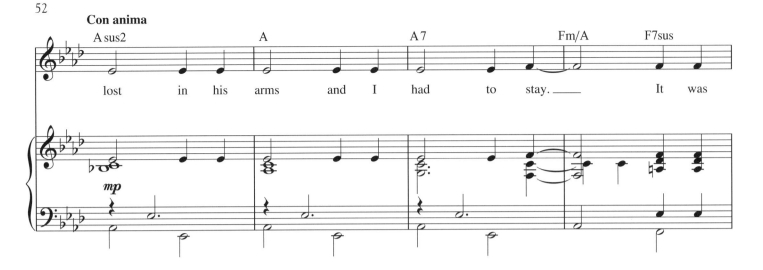

lost in his arms and I had to stay. ____ It was

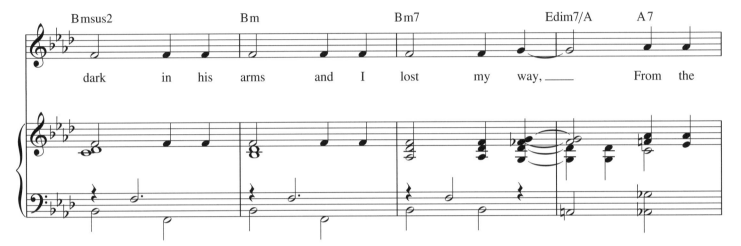

dark in his arms and I lost my way, ____ From the

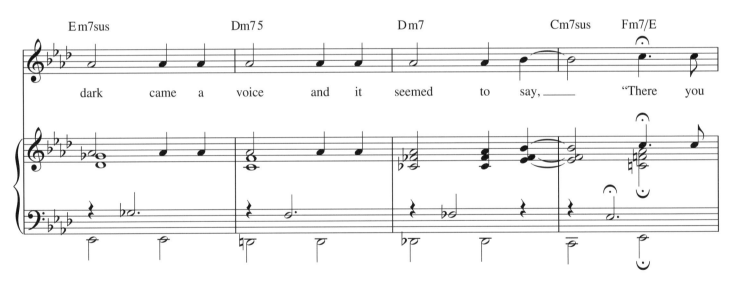

dark came a voice and it seemed to say, ____ "There you

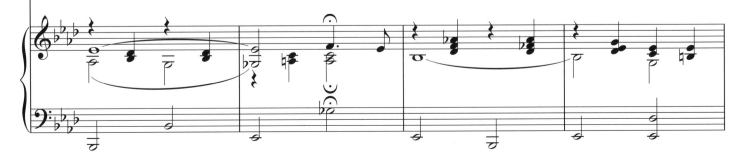

go, _____ There you go." _____ How I

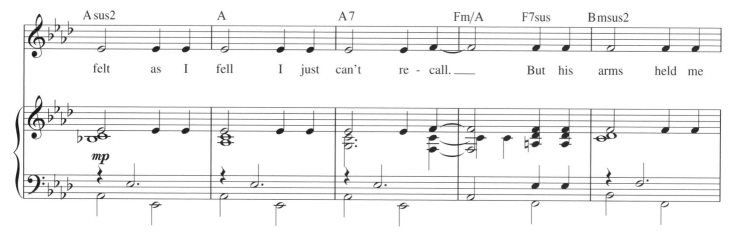

felt as I fell I just can't re-call. ___ But his arms held me

fast and it broke the fall. ___ And I said to my heart as it

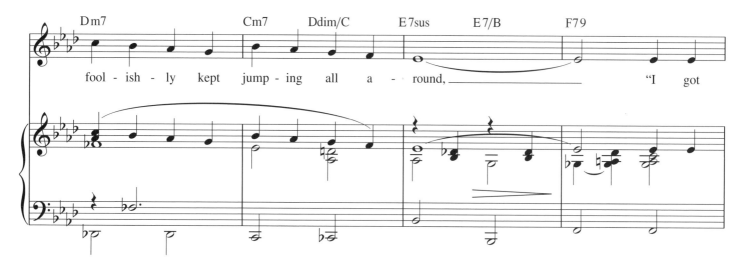

fool-ish-ly kept jump-ing all a-round, ___ "I got

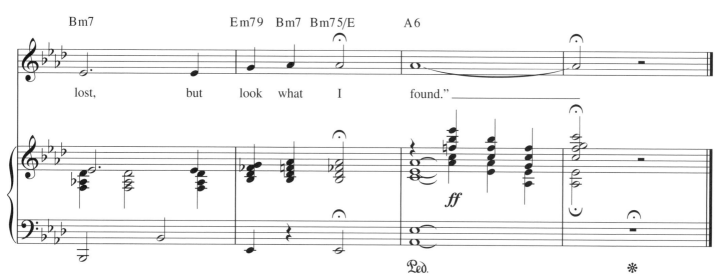

lost, but look what I found." ___

I Got It Bad and That Ain't Good

Words by PAUL FRANCIS WEBSTER
Music by DUKE ELLINGTON

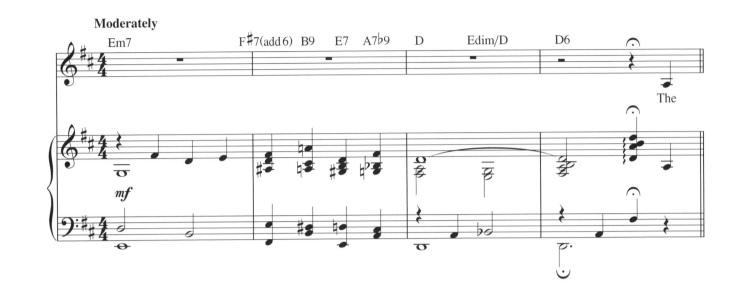

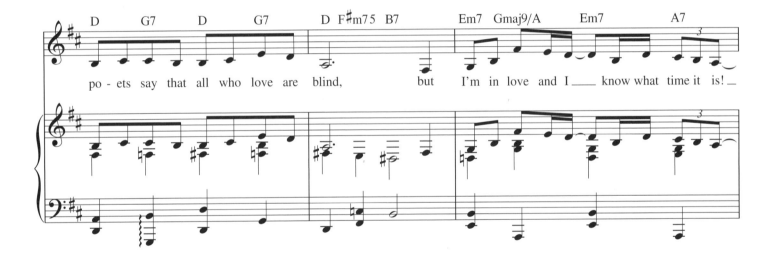

po - ets say that all who love are blind, but I'm in love and I ___ know what time it is!

The Good Book says, "Go seek and ye shall find." Well,

Moderately slow

Nev - er treats me sweet and gen - tle the way he should.
Like a lone - ly weep - ing wil - low lost in the wood,

I got it bad and that ain't good!
I got it bad and that ain't good!

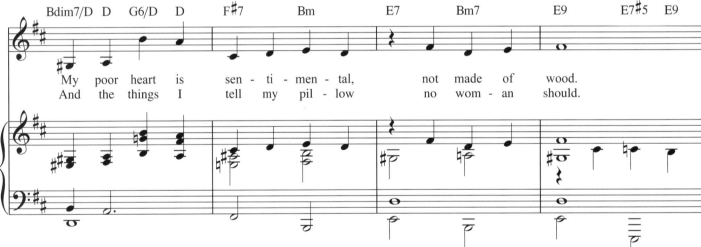

My poor heart is sen - ti - men - tal, not made of wood.
And the things I tell my pil - low no wom - an should.

I got it bad and that ain't good! But
I got it bad and that ain't good! Though

I Had Myself a True Love

from ST. LOUIS WOMAN

Words by JOHNNY MERCER
Music by HAROLD ARLEN

Slowly and with tenderness

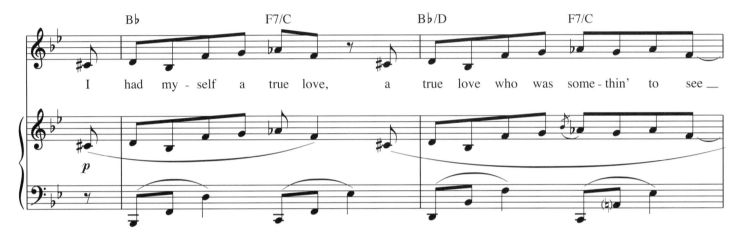

I had my-self a true love, a true love who was some-thin' to see __

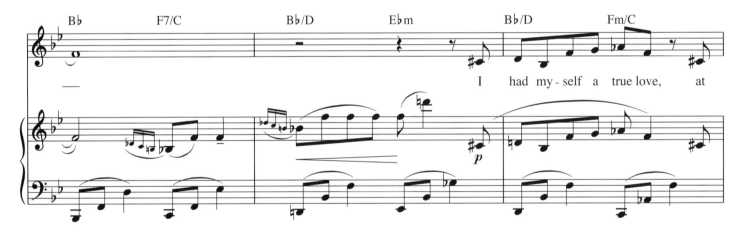

__ I had my-self a true love, at

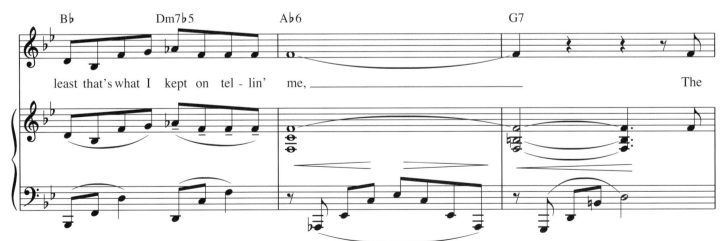

least that's what I kept on tel-lin' me, _____ The

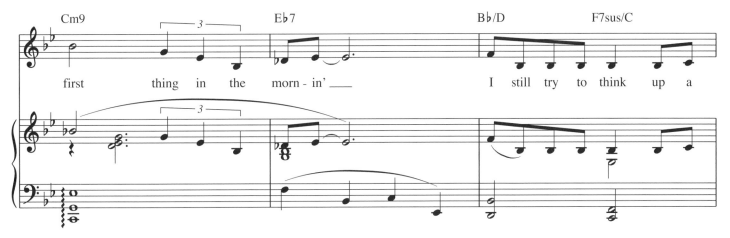

first thing in the morn - in' ___ I still try to think up a

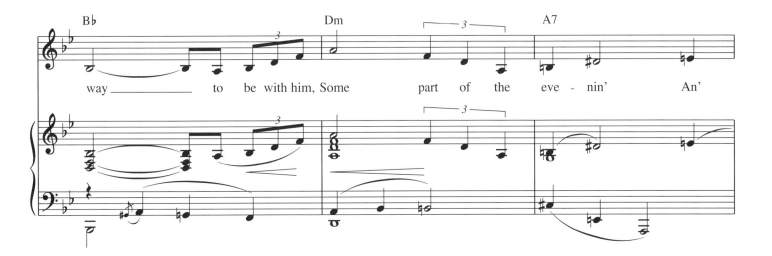

way _____ to be with him, Some part of the eve - nin' An'

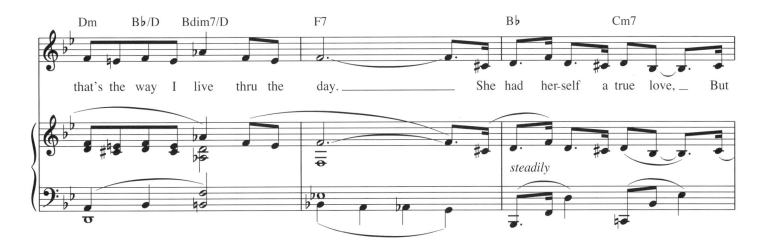

that's the way I live thru the day. _____ She had her-self a true love, ___ But

now he's gone an' left her for good. _____ The

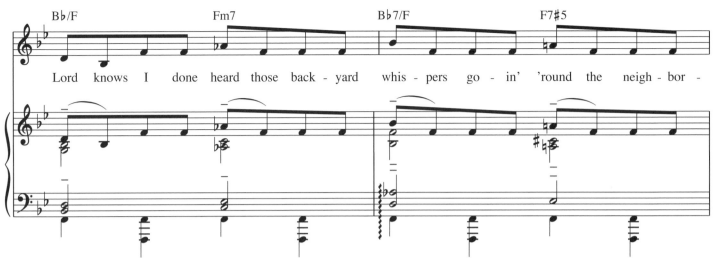

Lord knows I done heard those back - yard whis - pers go - in' 'round the neigh - bor -

hood. There may___ be a lot of

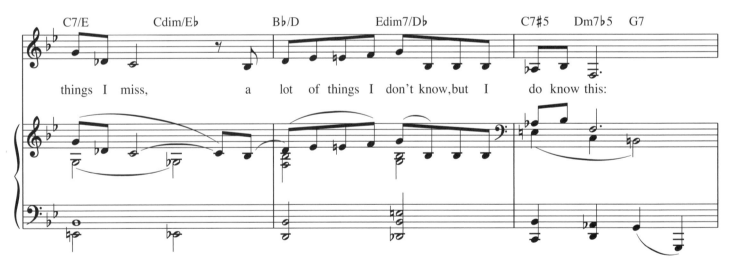

things I miss, a lot of things I don't know, but I do know this:

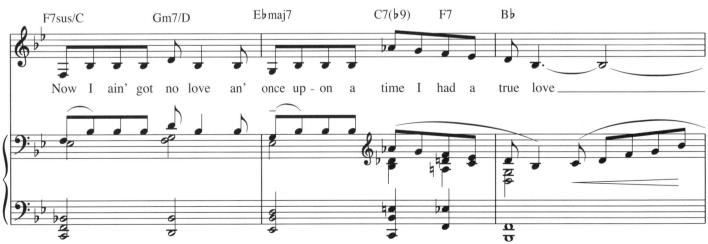

Now I ain' got no love an' once up - on a time I had a true love___

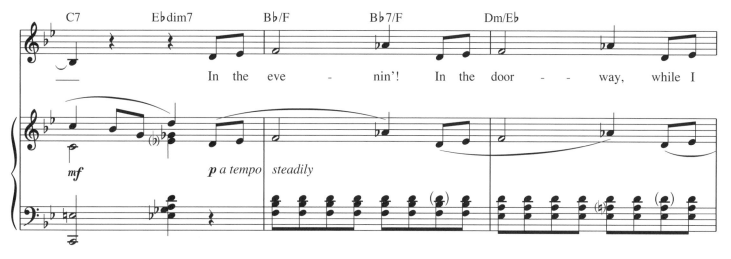

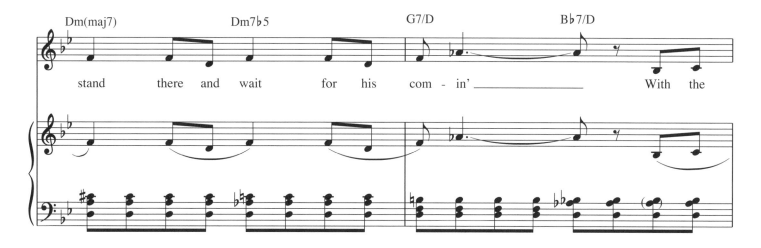

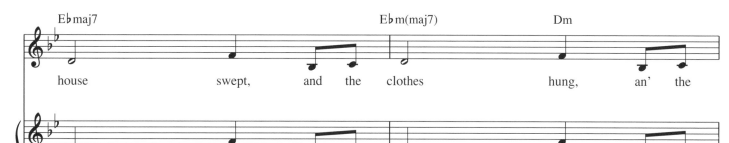

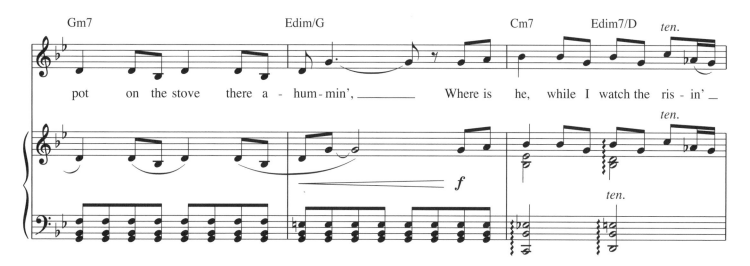

62

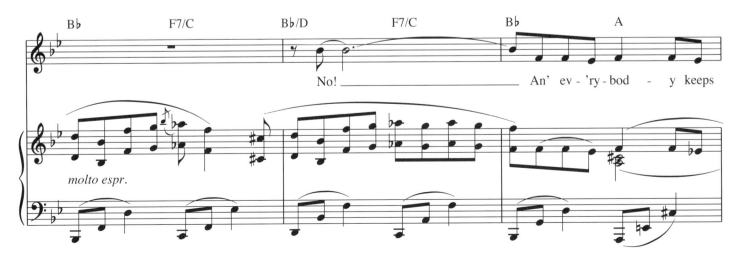

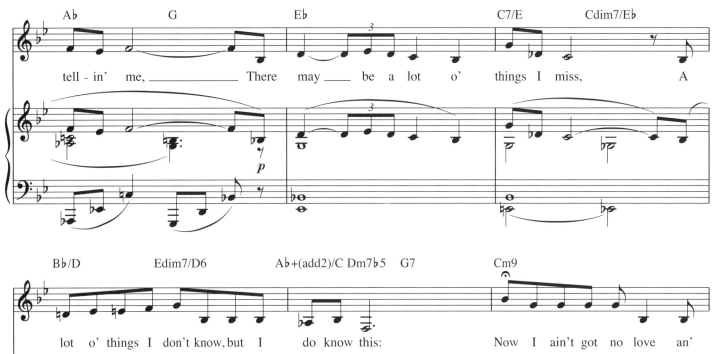

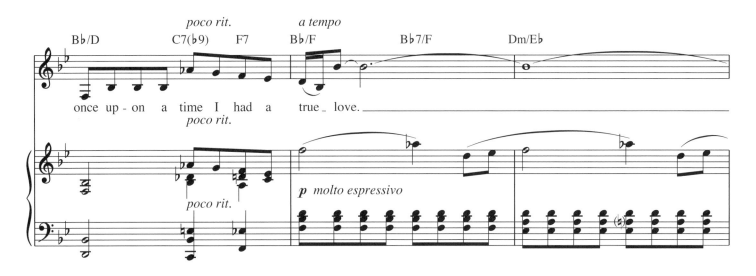

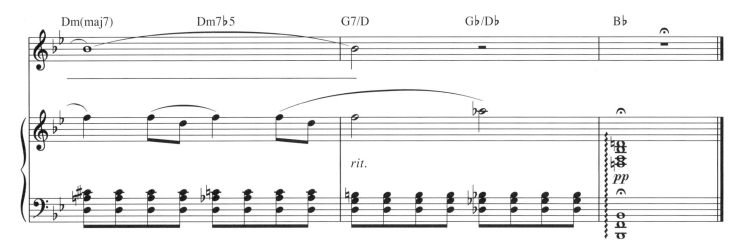

I Never Has Seen Snow

from HOUSE OF FLOWERS

Lyric by TRUMAN CAPOTE
and HAROLD ARLEN
Music by HAROLD ARLEN

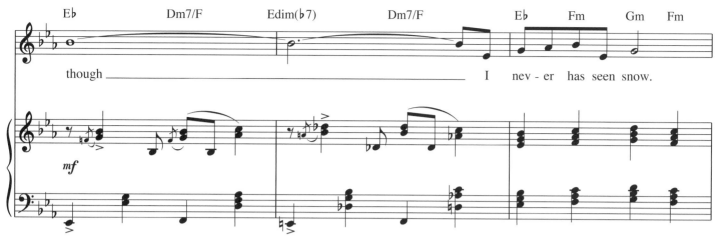

though _____ I nev - er has seen snow.

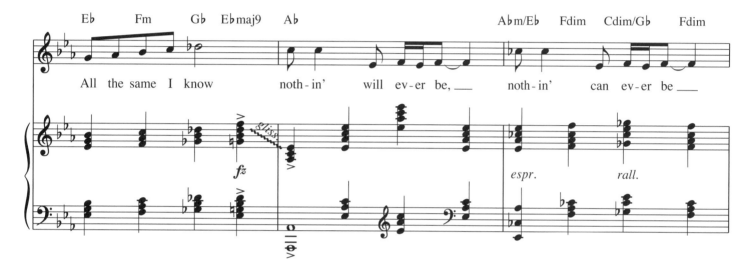

All the same I know noth - in' will ev - er be, ___ noth - in' can ev - er be ___

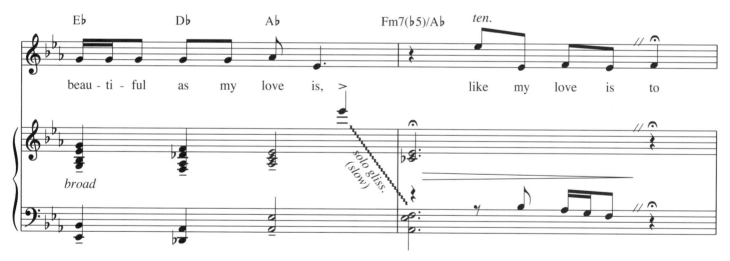

beau - ti - ful as my love is, > like my love is to

me. _____

I Wish I Were in Love Again

from BABES IN ARMS

Words by LORENZ HART
Music by RICHARD RODGERS

This is a duet in the show, adapted here as a solo.

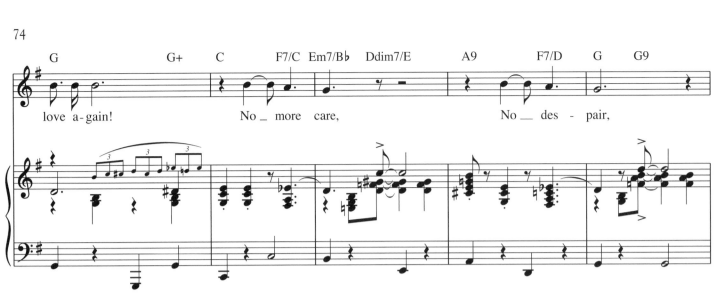

love a-gain! No _ more care, No _ des - pair,

I'm _ all there now, _ But I'd rath - er be punch drunk!_ Be -

lieve me, sir, I much pre - fer the clas - sic bat - tle of a him and her, I

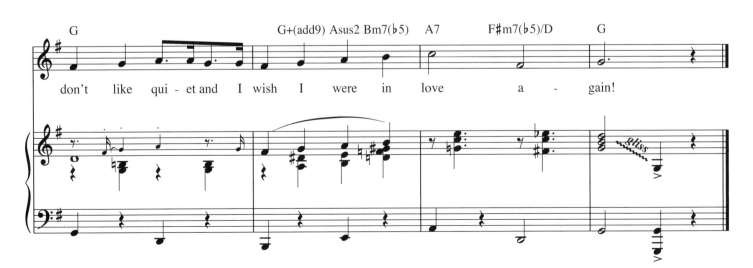

don't like qui - et and I wish I were in love a - gain!

I'm Still Here

from FOLLIES

Music and Lyrics by
STEPHEN SONDHEIM

I've stuffed the dail - ies___ In my___ shoes,___

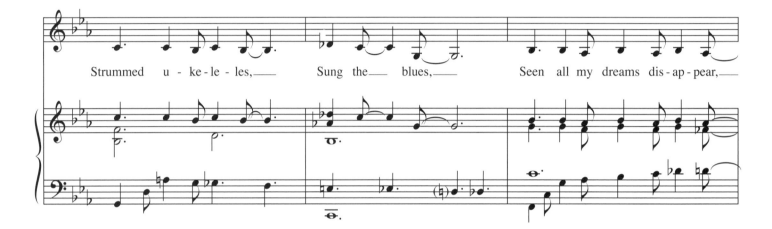

Strummed u - ke - le - les,___ Sung the___ blues,___ Seen all my dreams dis - ap - pear,___

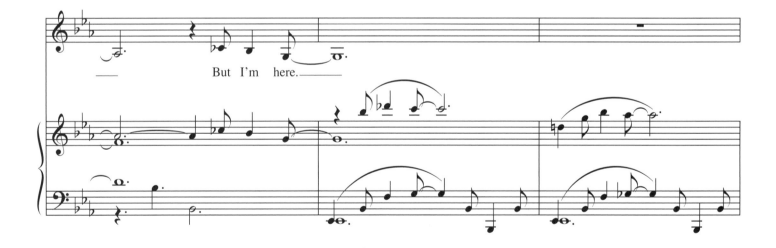

But I'm here.___

I've slept in shan - ties, Guest of the W.___ P. A.,___ But I'm here.

Danced in my scan-ties,_____ Three bucks a night was the pay,_____

_____ But I'm here._____ I've stood in bread-lines_____

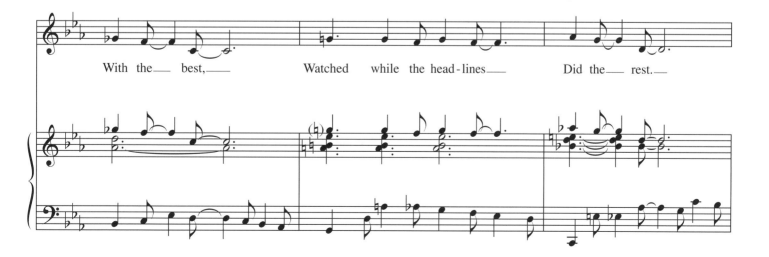

With the__ best,__ Watched while the head-lines__ Did the__ rest.__

In the De - pres - sion was I___ de - pressed?___ No-where

dim.

near.___

I met a big fi - nan - cier,___ And I'm

mp

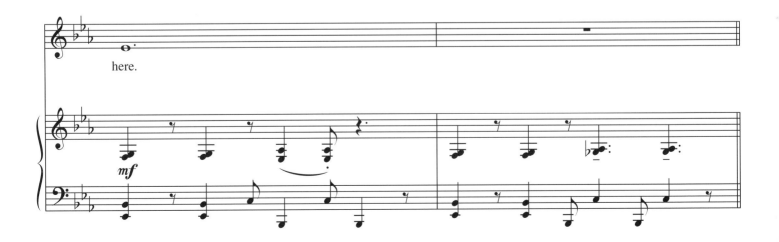

here.

mf

I've been through Gand-hi,_____ Wind-sor and Wal-ly's af-fair,_____ And I'm here._____

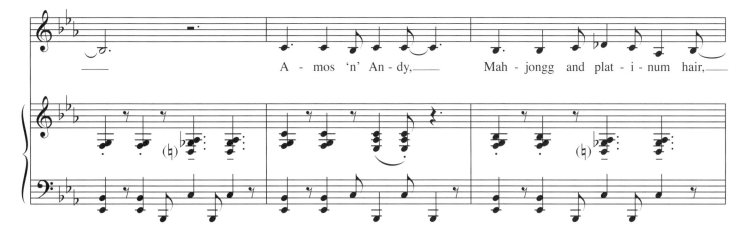

_____ A - mos 'n' An - dy,_____ Mah - jongg and plat - i - num hair,_____

_____ And I'm here._____ I got through A - bie's_____

I - rish_____ Rose,_____ Five Di - onne ba - bies,_____ Ma - jor_____ Bowes,

Had hee-bie-jee-bies___ For Bee-be's___ Bath-y - sphere.___

I lived through Bren-da___ Fra - zier___ And I'm

here._____ I've got-ten through

Her - bert and J. Ed-gar Hoo - ver,___

Gee, that was fun___ and a half.___ When you've been through

Her - bert and J. Ed - gar Hoo - ver,___

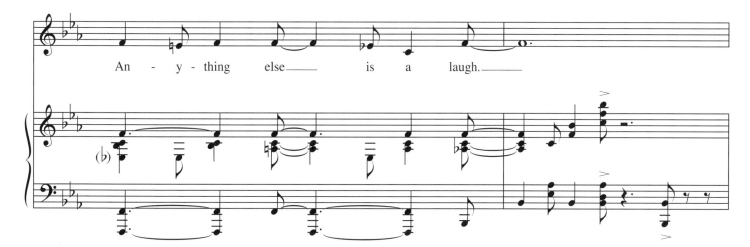

An - y - thing else___ is a laugh.___

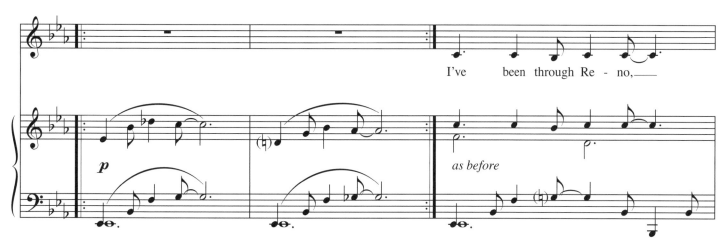

I've been through Re - no,___

I've been through Bev - er - ly Hills,_____ And I'm here._____

Reef - ers and vin - o,_____ Rest cures, re - li - gion and pills,_____

_____ But I'm here._____

Been called a pink - o_____ Com - mie_____ tool,_____ Got through it stink - o_____

poco cresc.

mp

By my pool. I should have gone to an act - ing school, That seems

clear. Still some - one said, "She's sin - cere,"

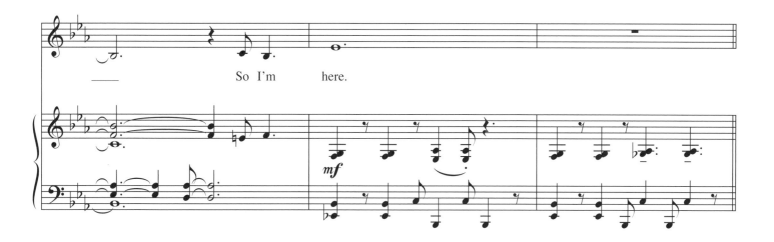

So I'm here.

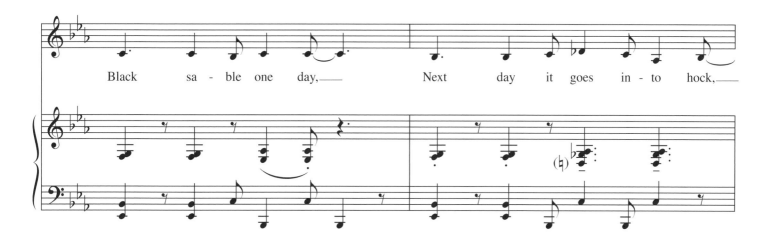

Black sa - ble one day, Next day it goes in - to hock,

to ca - reer.

I'm al - most through my___ mem - oirs,___ And I'm

here.___ I've got - ten through

"Hey, la - dy, are - n't you whoo - zis?___

Plush vel - vet some - times,___ Some - times just pret - zels and beer,___

But I'm here.___ I've run the gam - ut,___

A to___ Z.___ Three cheers and dam - mit,___ *C'est la___ vie.*___

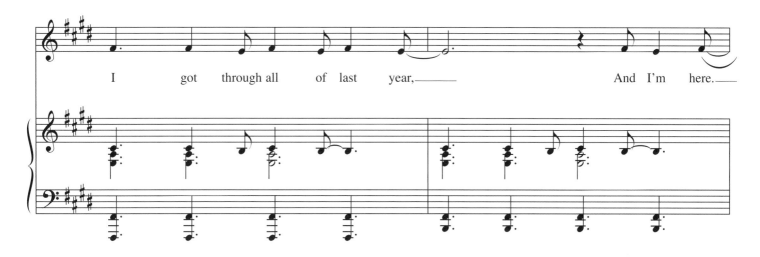

I got through all of last year,___ And I'm here.___

Lord knows, at least I've been there,_____ And I'm here!_____

_____ Look who's here!_____ I'm still

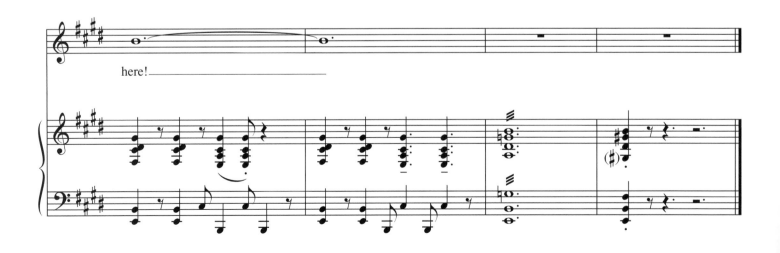

here!_____

If He Walked Into My Life

from MAME

Music and Lyric by
JERRY HERMAN

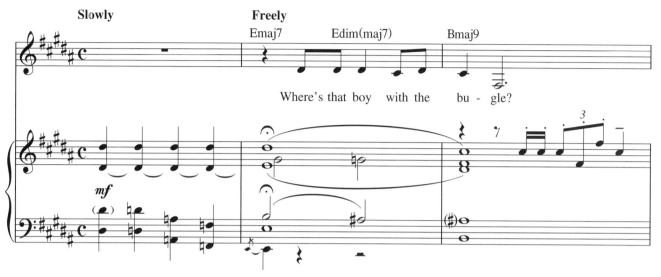

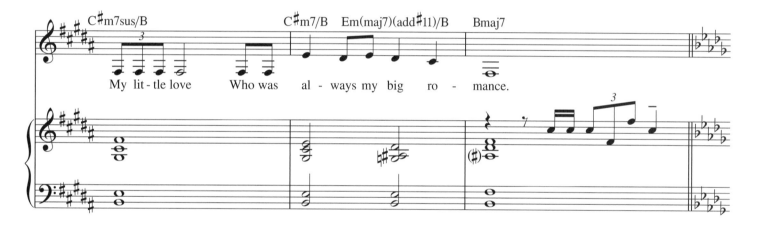

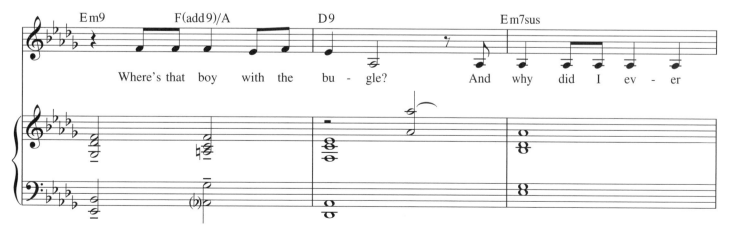

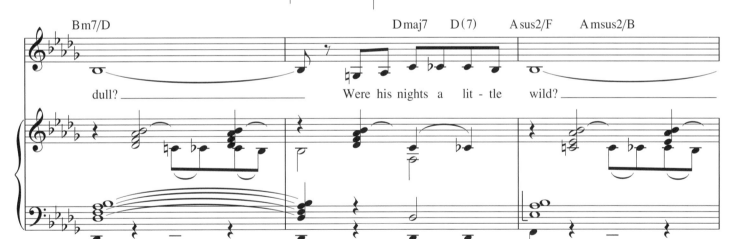

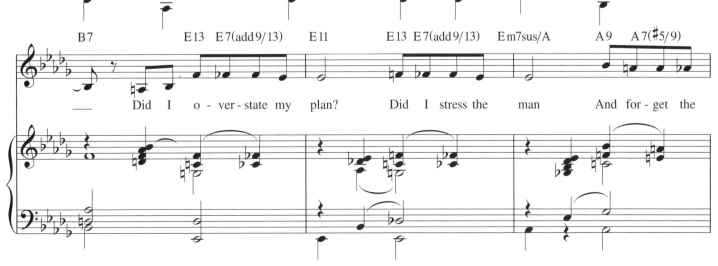

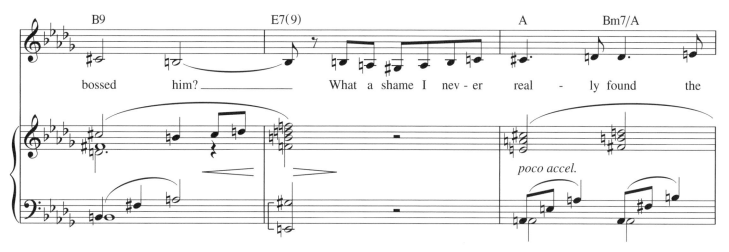

bossed him? _____ What a shame I nev-er real - ly found the

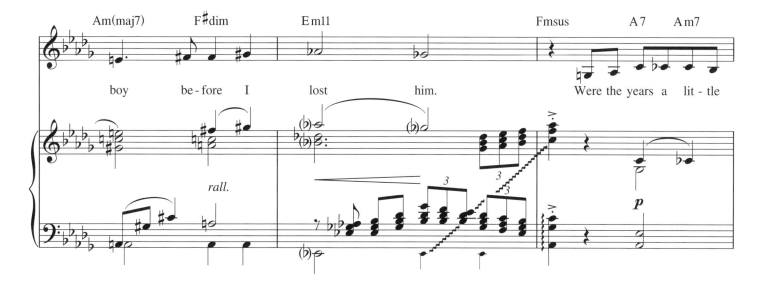

boy be - fore I lost him. Were the years a lit - tle

fast? _____ Was his world a lit - tle free? _____

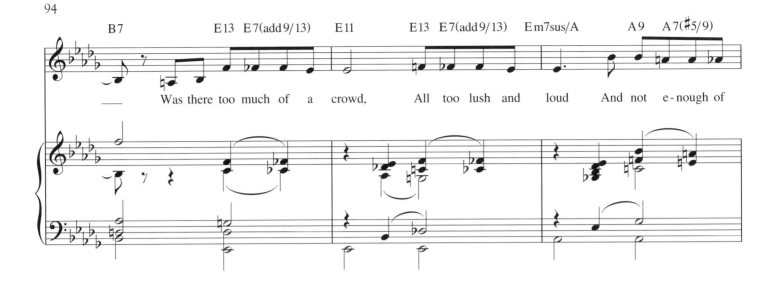

Was there too much of a crowd, All too lush and loud And not e-nough of

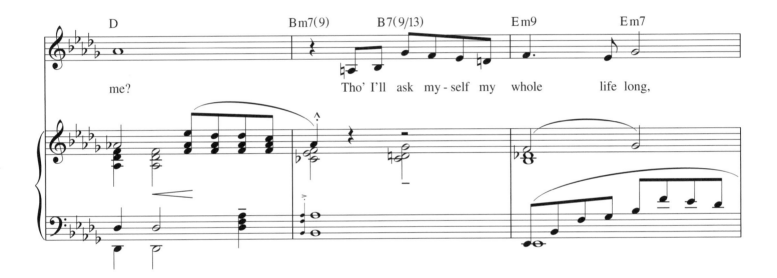

me? Tho' I'll ask my-self my whole life long,

What went wrong a-long the way? _____ Would I make the same mis-

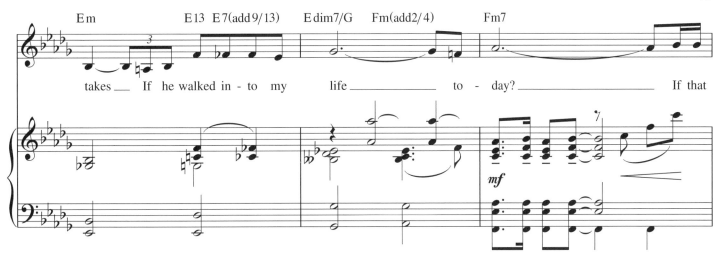

takes ___ If he walked in-to my life _____ to - day? _____ If that

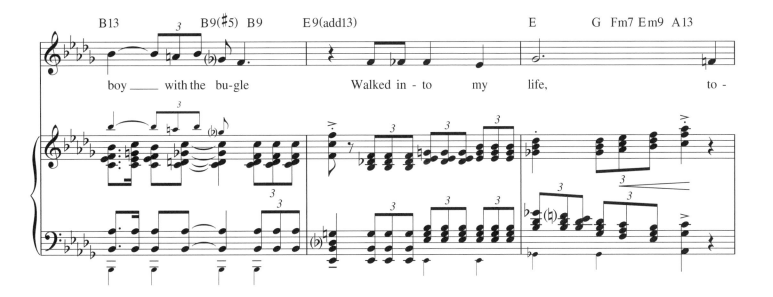

boy ____ with the bu-gle Walked in - to my life, to -

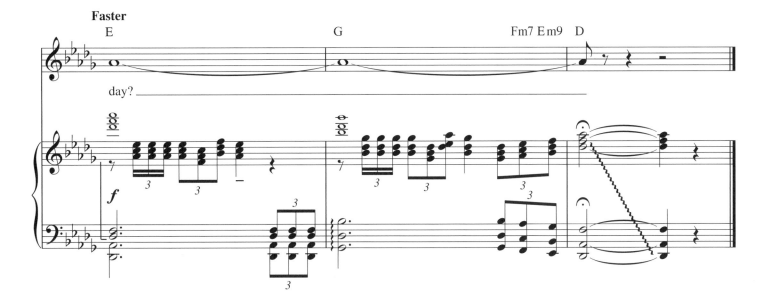

Faster

day? _____

In a Sentimental Mood

Words and Music by DUKE ELLINGTON,
IRVING MILLS and MANNY KURTZ

Slowly, with expression

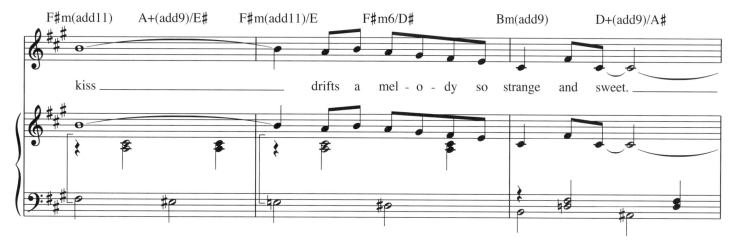

Keepin' Out of Mischief Now

Lyric by ANDY RAZAF
Music by THOMAS "FATS" WALLER

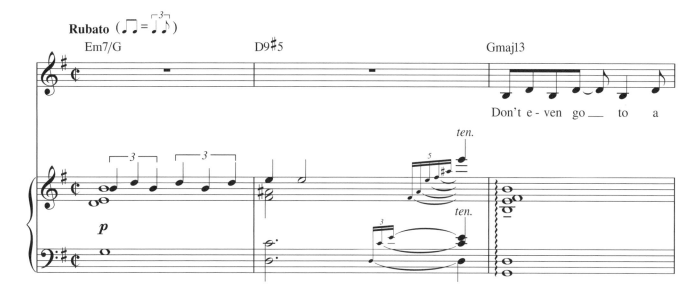

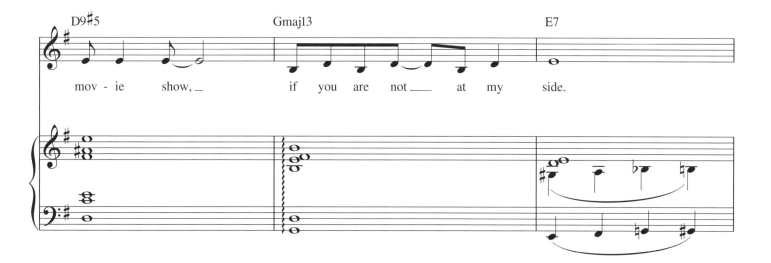

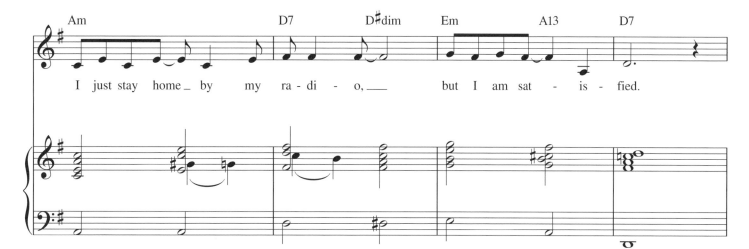

ny. All my op - in - ions have changed some - how, ___

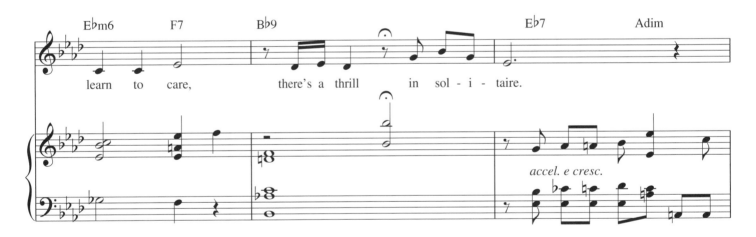

Rubato

old fash - ioned as ___ can be. When you real - ly

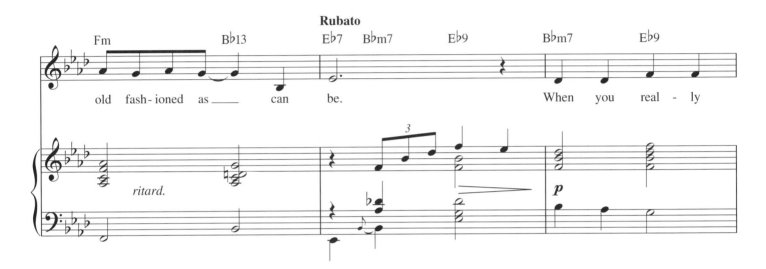

learn to care, there's a thrill in sol - i - taire.

Tempo I

All the world can plain - ly see, you're the on - ly one for

The Lady Is a Tramp

from BABES IN ARMS

Words by LORENZ HART
Music by RICHARD RODGERS

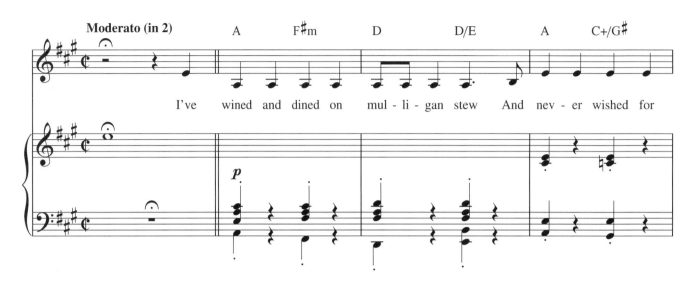

I've wined and dined on mul-li-gan stew And nev-er wished for

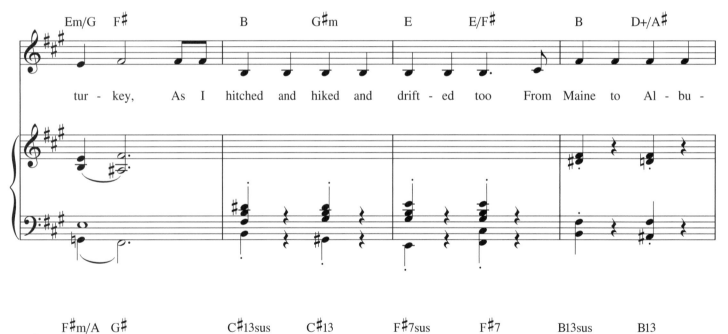

tur-key, As I hitched and hiked and drift-ed too From Maine to Al-bu-

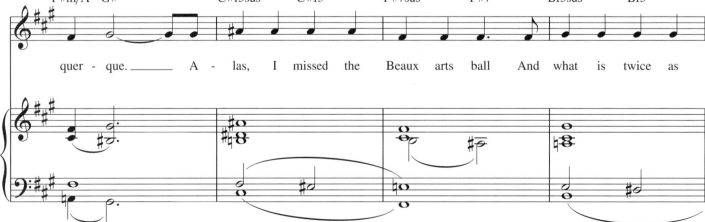

quer-que.___ A-las, I missed the Beaux arts ball And what is twice as

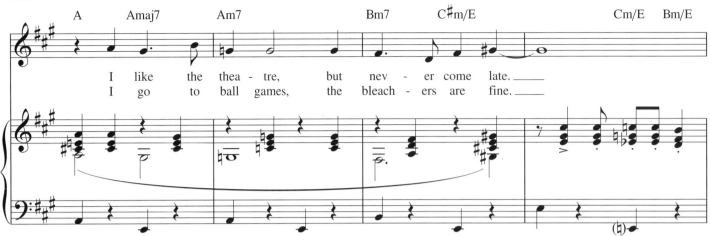

I like the thea - tre, but nev - er come late. ____
I go to ball games, the bleach - ers are fine. ____

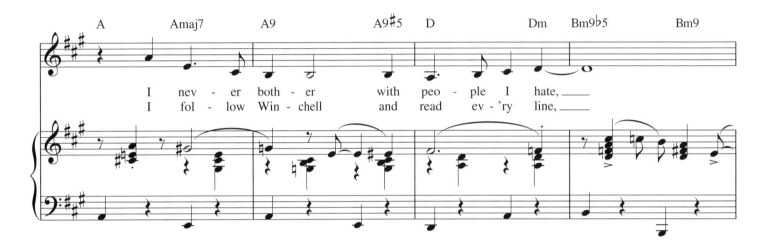

I nev - er both - er with peo - ple I hate, ____
I fol - low Win - chell and read ev - 'ry line, ____

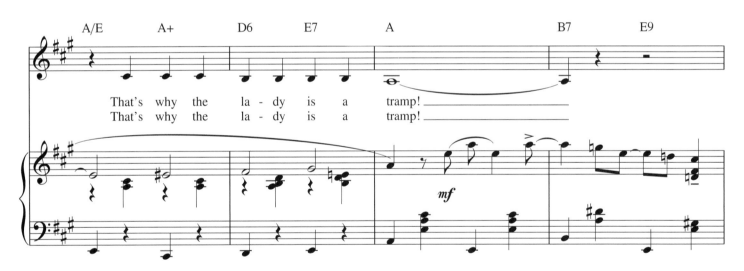

That's why the la - dy is a tramp! ____
That's why the la - dy is a tramp! ____

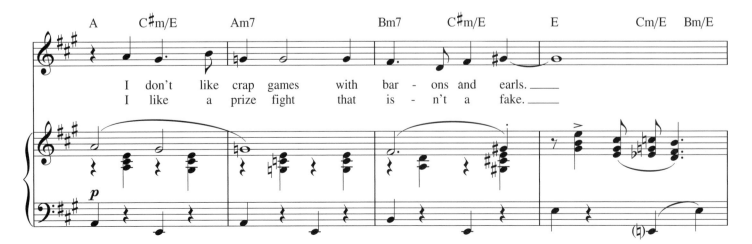

I don't like crap games with bar - ons and earls. ____
I like a prize fight that is - n't a fake. ____

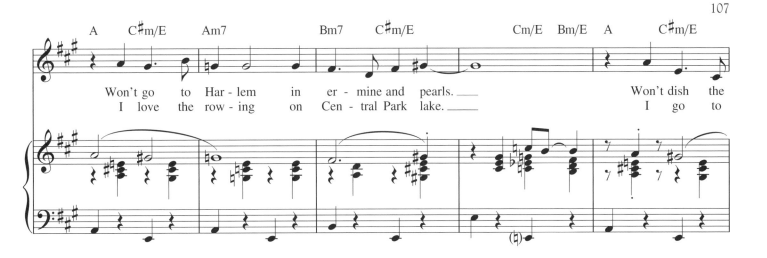

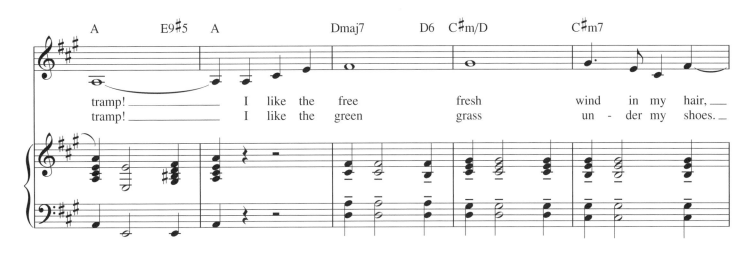

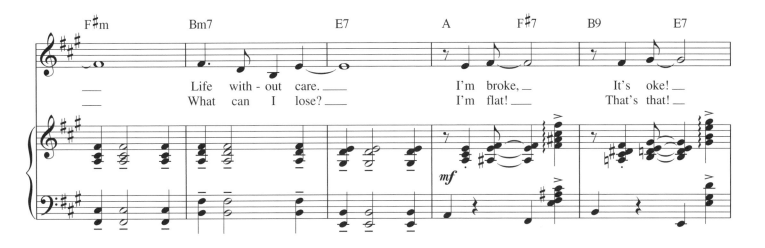

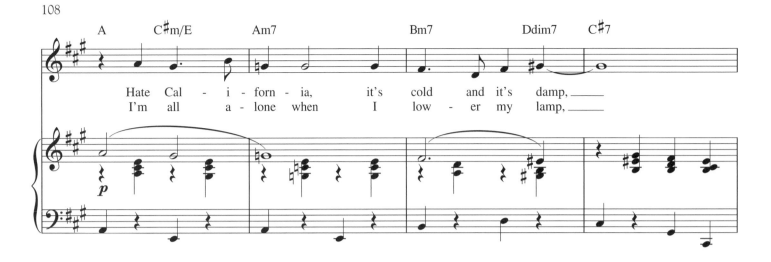

Hate Cal - i - forn - ia, it's cold and it's damp, _____
I'm all a - lone when I low - er my lamp, _____

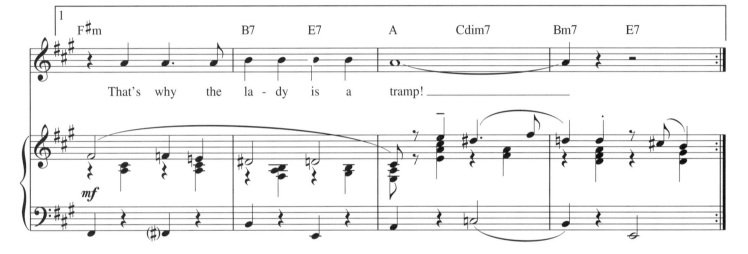

That's why the la - dy is a tramp! _____

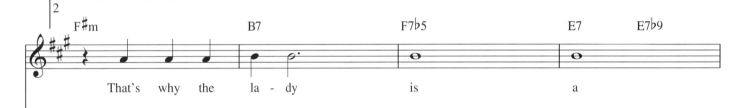

That's why the la - dy is a

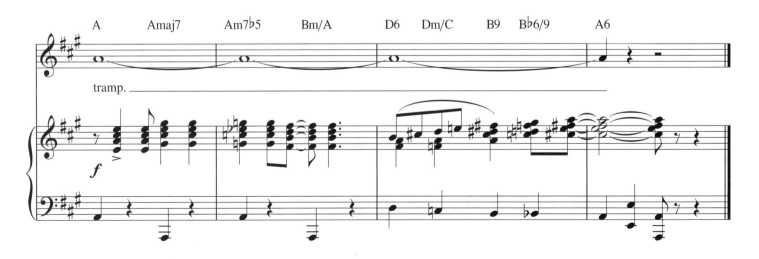

tramp. _____

Long Ago
(And Far Away)
from COVER GIRL

Words by IRA GERSHWIN
Music by JEROME KERN

Burthen (*cantabile*)

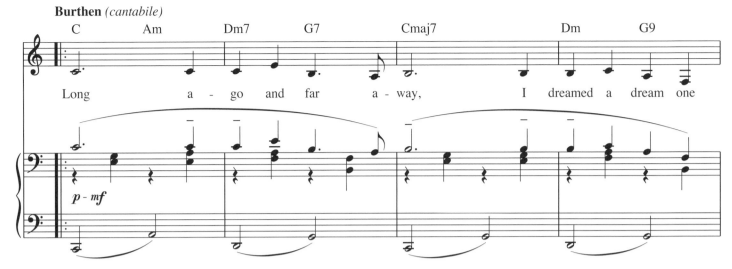

Long a - go and far a - way, I dreamed a dream one

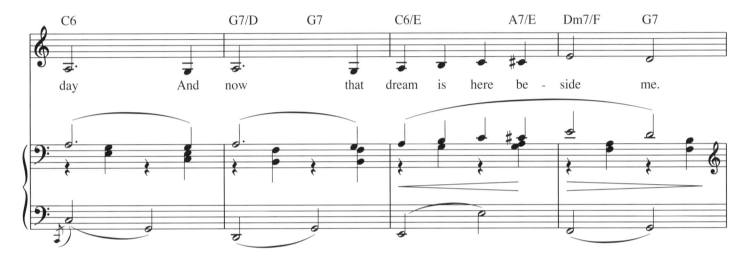

day And now that dream is here be - side me.

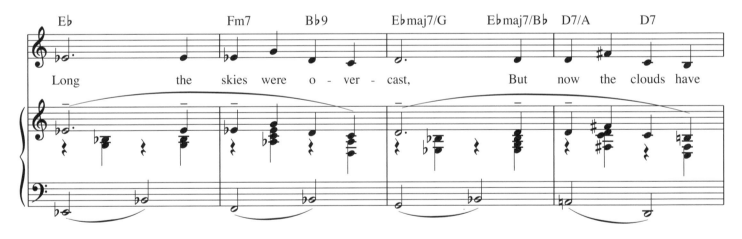

Long the skies were o - ver - cast, But now the clouds have

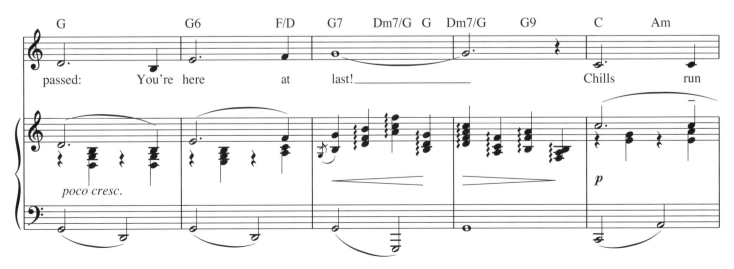

passed: You're here at last! Chills run

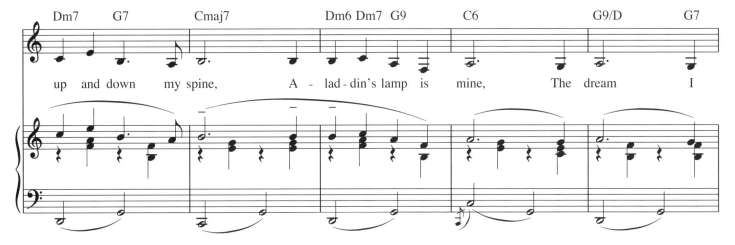

up and down my spine, A-lad-din's lamp is mine, The dream I

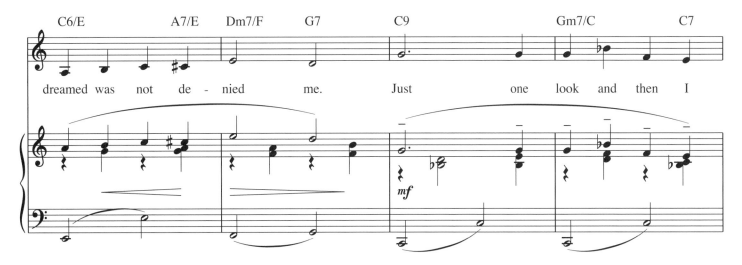

dreamed was not de-nied me. Just one look and then I

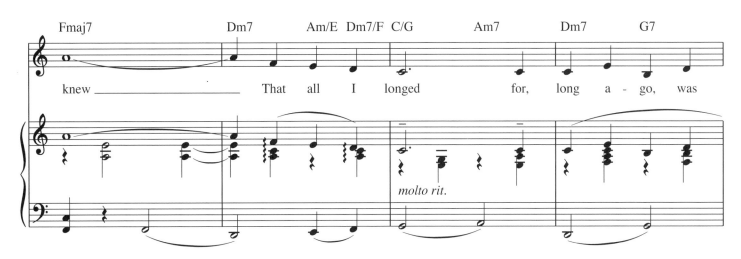

knew _____ That all I longed for, long a-go, was

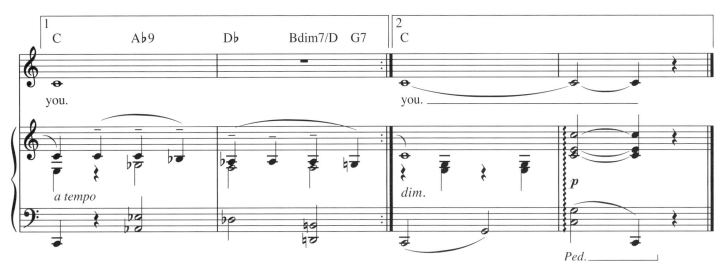

you.

you.

Love Me or Leave Me

from LOVE ME OR LEAVE ME

Lyrics by GUS KAHN
Music by WALTER DONALDSON

This sus-pense _____ is kill-ing me _____

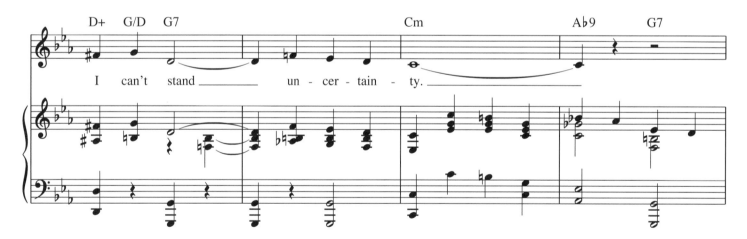

I can't stand _____ un-cer-tain-ty.

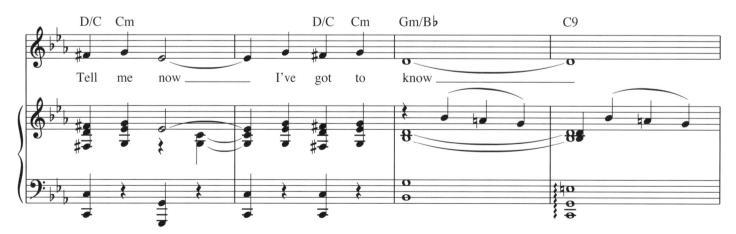

Tell me now _____ I've got to know _____

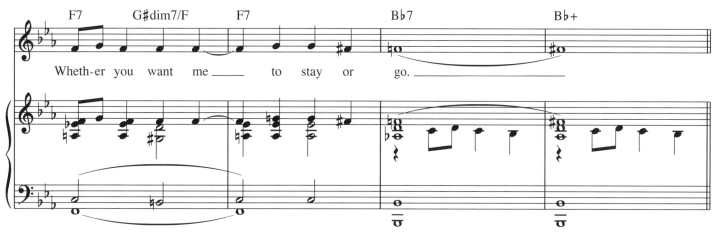

Wheth-er you want me ___ to stay or go. ___

Love me or leave me and let me be lone-ly, You won't be-lieve me, and

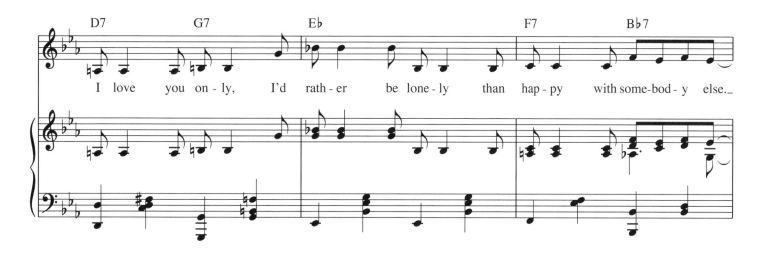

I love you on-ly, I'd rath-er be lone-ly than hap-py with some-bod-y else.

You

might find the night-time the right time for kiss-ing, But night-time is my time for

just rem - i - nisc-ing, Re - gret-ting in-stead of for - get-ting with some-bod-y else.

There'll be no _____ one un -

less that some - one is you _____ I in-tend _ to be

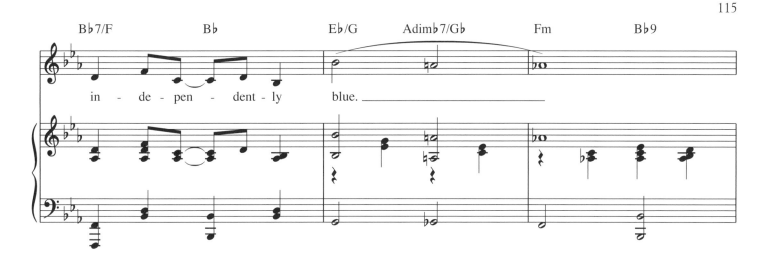

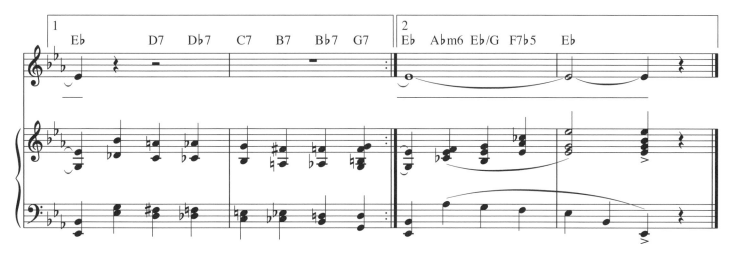

Make Someone Happy

from DO RE MI

Words by BETTY COMDEN and ADOLPH GREEN
Music by JULE STYNE

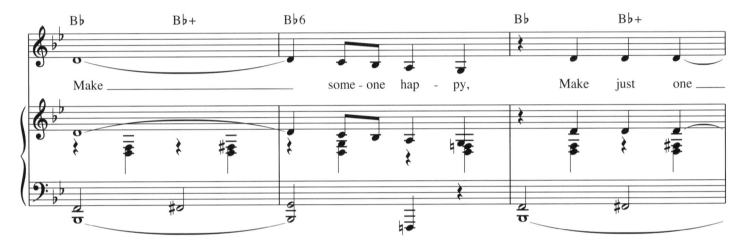

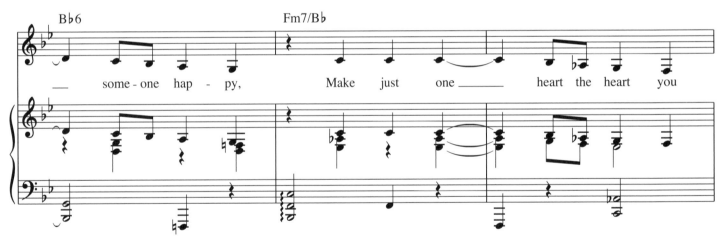

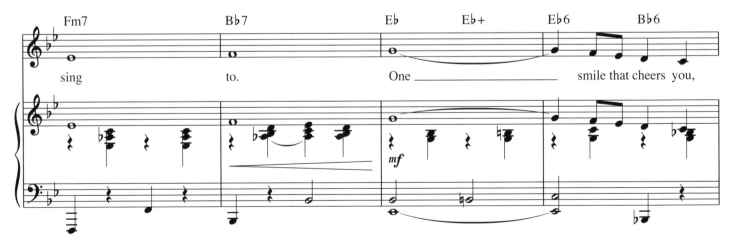

One face that lights when it nears you, One {man/girl} you're

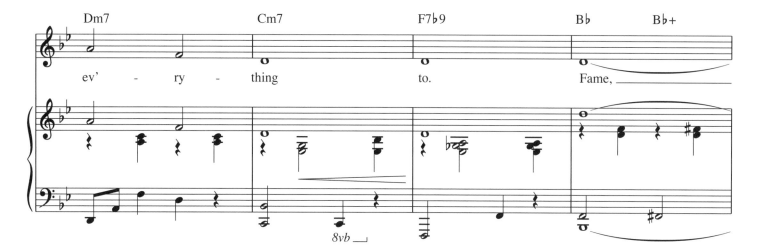

ev' - ry - thing to. Fame, _____

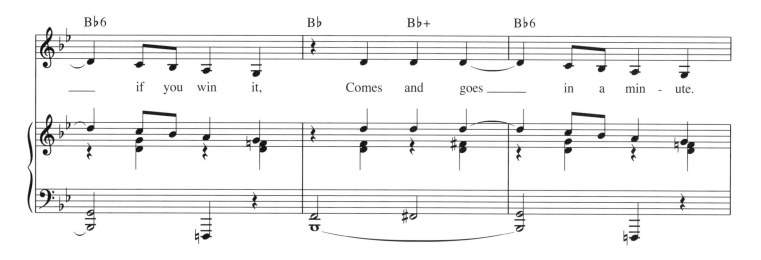

_____ if you win it, Comes and goes _____ in a min - ute.

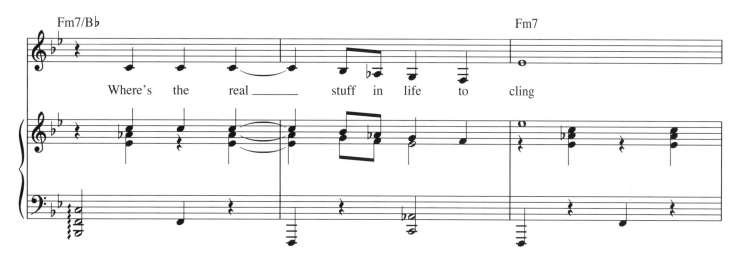

Where's the real _____ stuff in life to cling

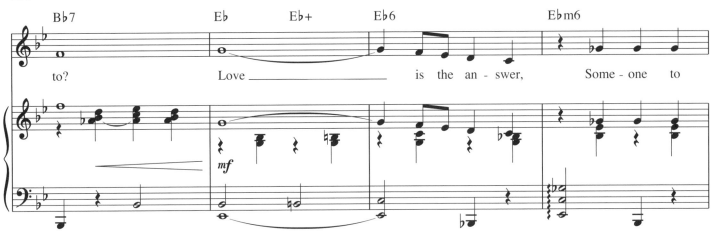

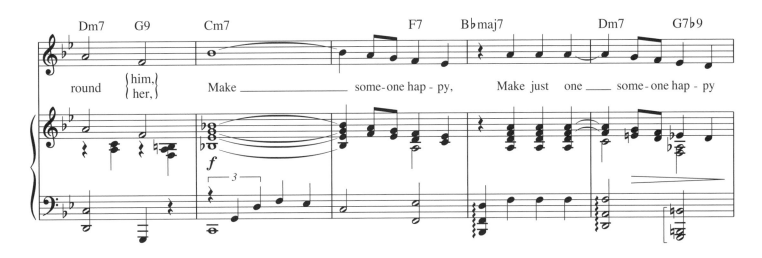

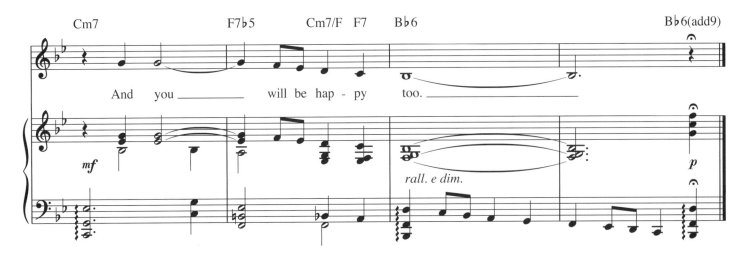

Maybe This Time

from CABARET

Words by FRED EBB
Music by JOHN KANDER

way. He will hold me fast.

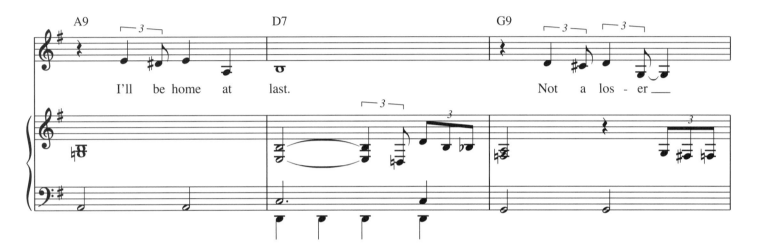

I'll be home at last. Not a los - er ___

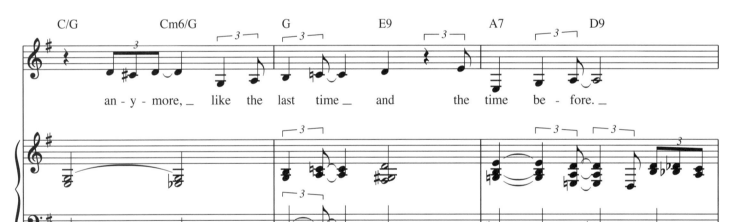

an - y - more, ___ like the last time ___ and the time be - fore. ___

Ev - 'ry-bod - y ___ loves a win - ner ___ so no-bod - y ___ loved

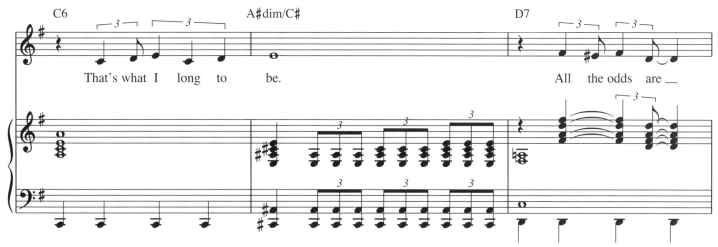

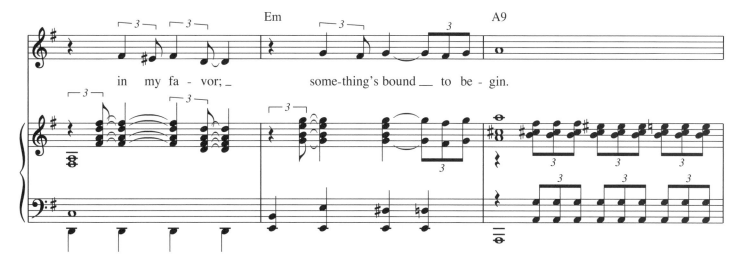

121

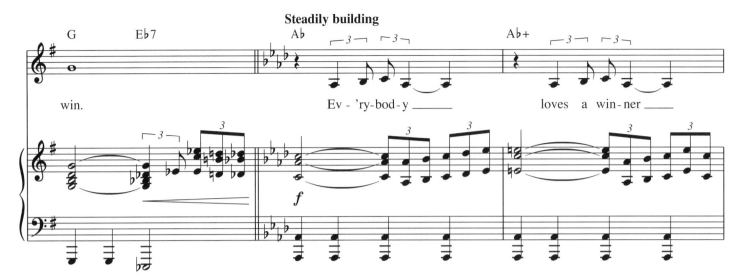

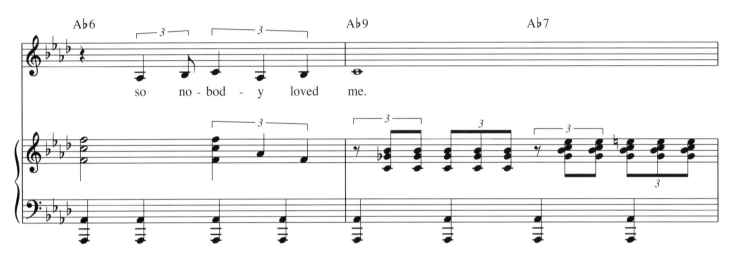

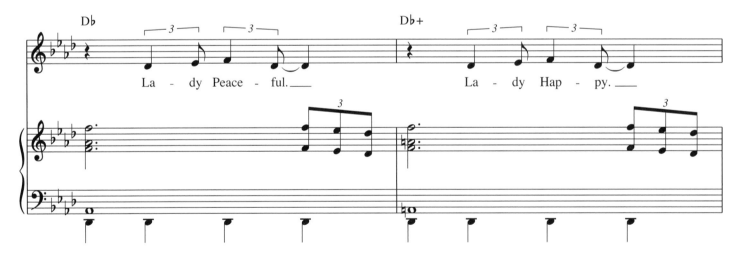

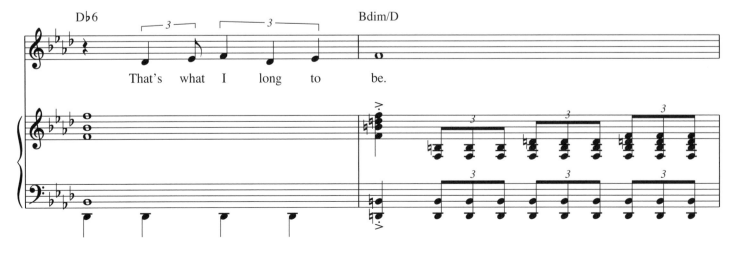

* In the 1998 Broadway Revival this final section was performed in an understated, soft way.

The Man That Got Away

from the Motion Picture A STAR IS BORN

Lyric by IRA GERSHWIN
Music by HAROLD ARLEN

Slowly, but insistently

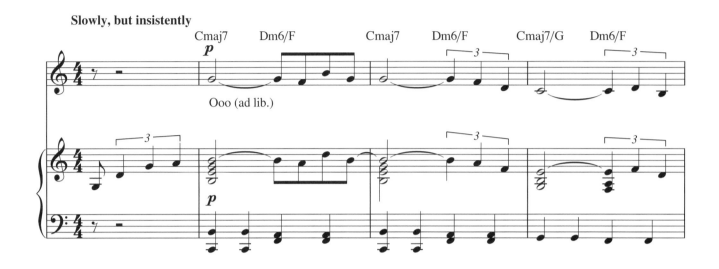

Ooo (ad lib.)

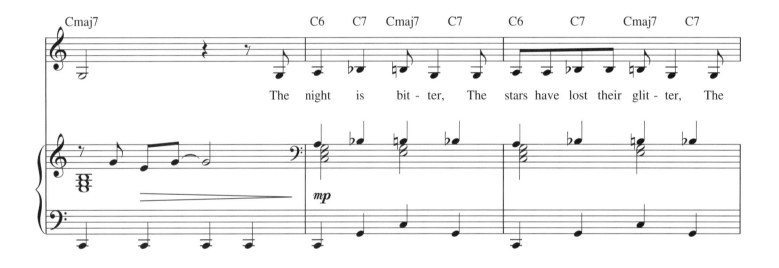

The night is bit - ter, The stars have lost their glit - ter, The

winds grow cold - er And sud - den - ly you're old - er And all be - cause of the

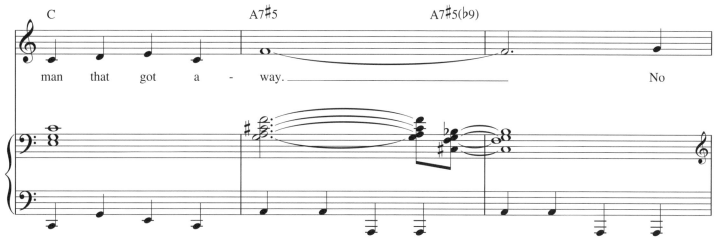

C   A7#5   A7#5(♭9)

man that got a - way. _____ No

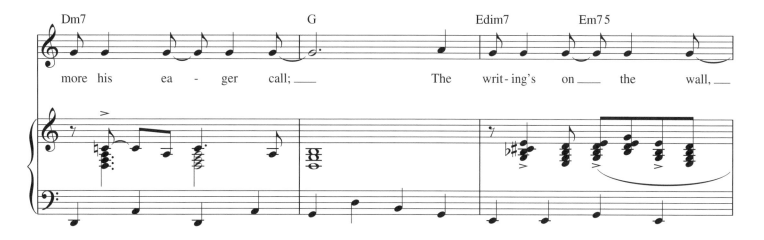

Dm7   G   Edim7   Em7♭5

more his ea - ger call; ___ The writ-ing's on ___ the wall, ___

A7♭9sus   Dm11   G7

___ The dreams you dream'd have all _____ gone a -

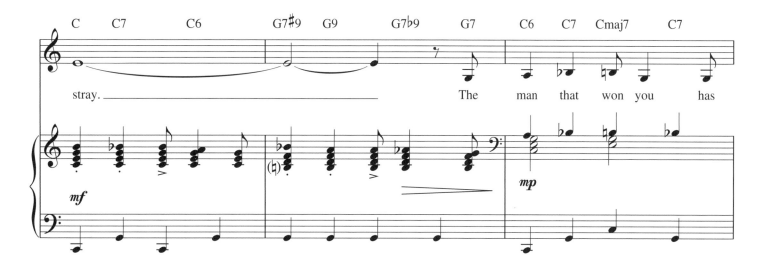

C   C7   C6   G7#9   G9   G7♭9   G7   C6   C7   Cmaj7   C7

stray. _____ The man that won you has

mf   mp

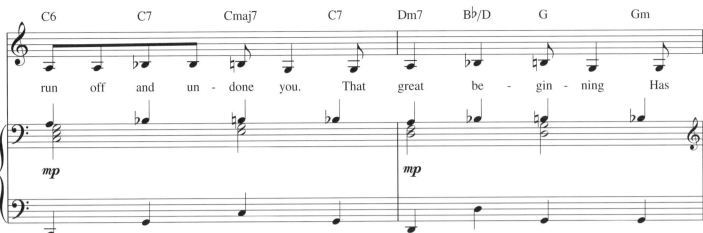

run off and un-done you. That great be - gin - ning Has

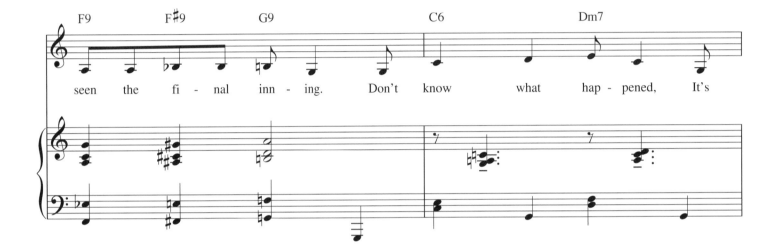

seen the fi - nal inn - ing. Don't know what hap - pened, It's

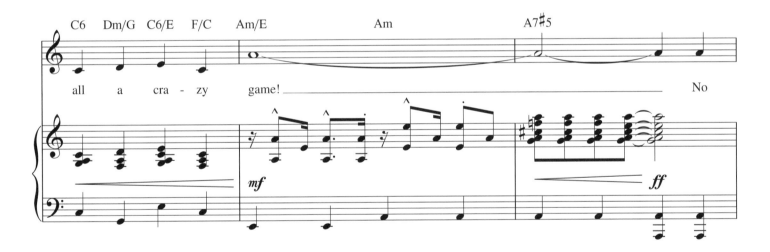

all a cra - zy game! No

more that all - time thrill, For you've been through the

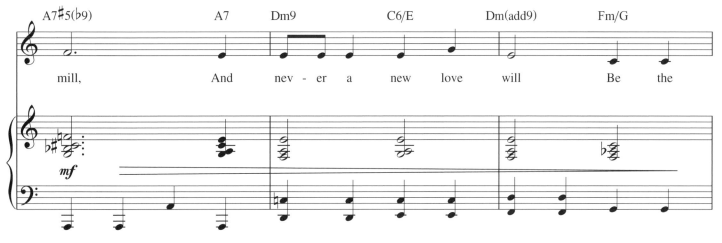

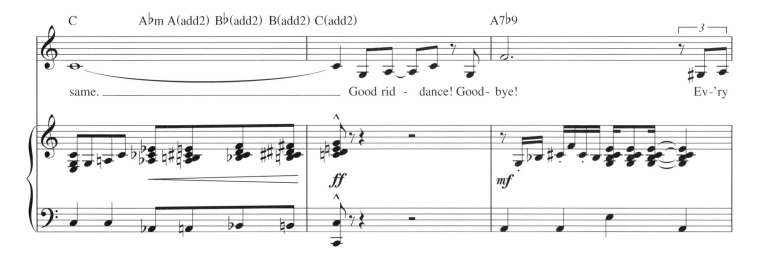

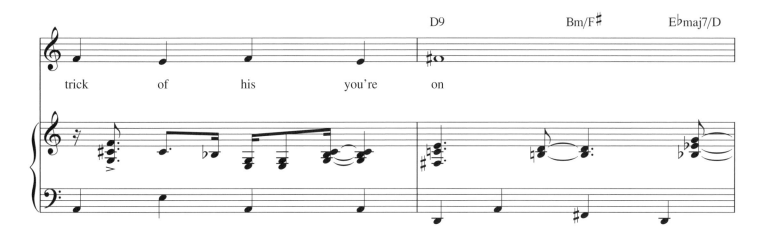

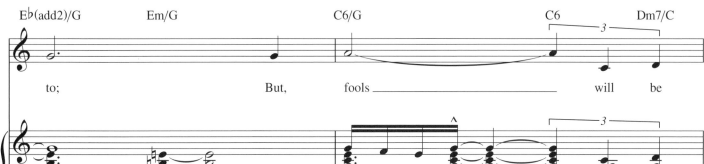

More Than You Know

Words by WILLIAM ROSE and EDWARD ELISCU
Music by VINCENT YOUMANS

Slowly, with expression

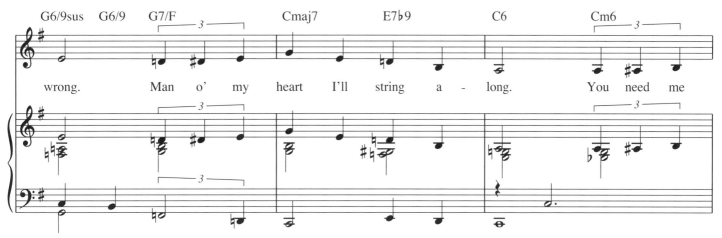

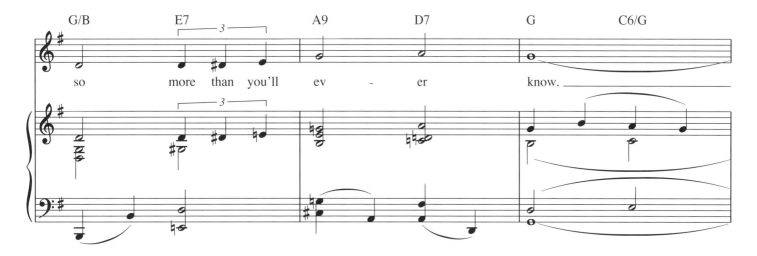

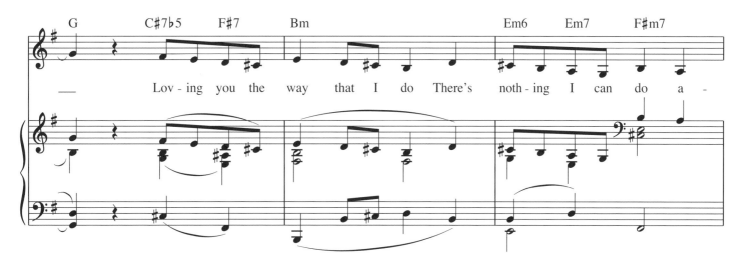

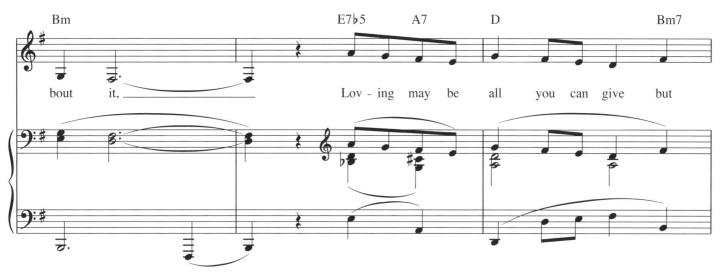

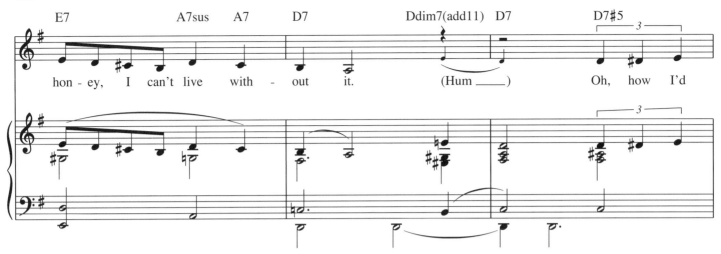

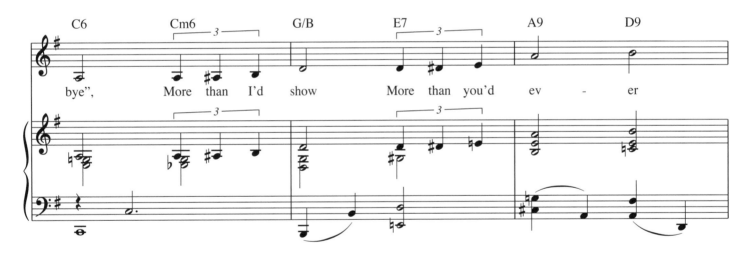

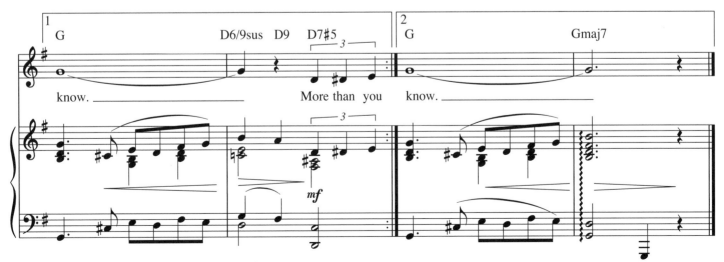

Nowadays

from CHICAGO

Words by FRED EBB
Music by JOHN KANDER

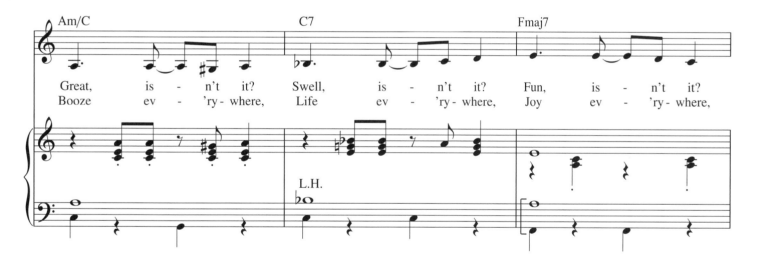

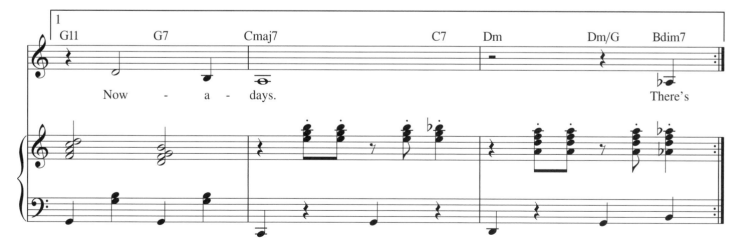

This song is a duet for Velma and Roxie in the show, adapted here as a solo.

134

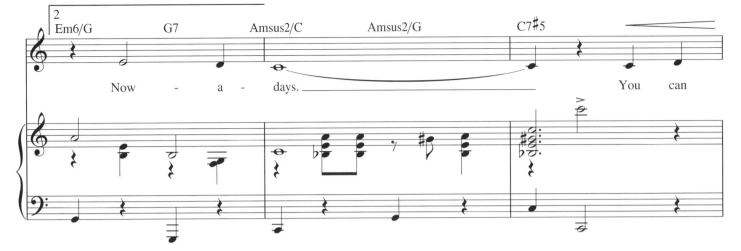

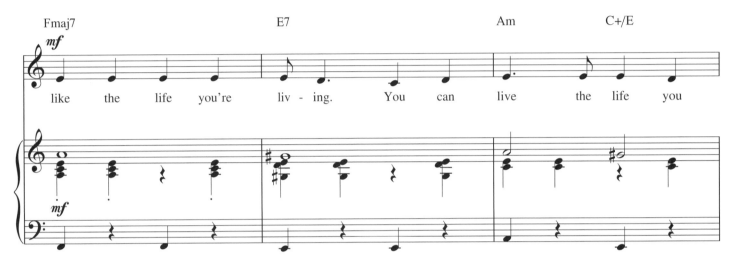

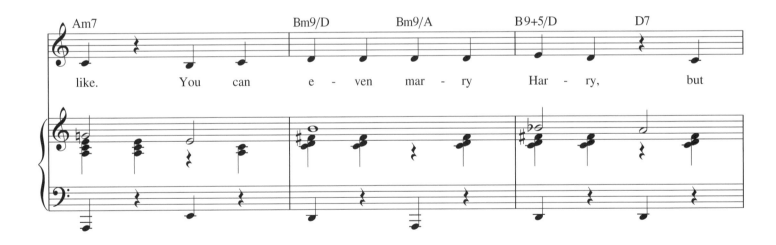

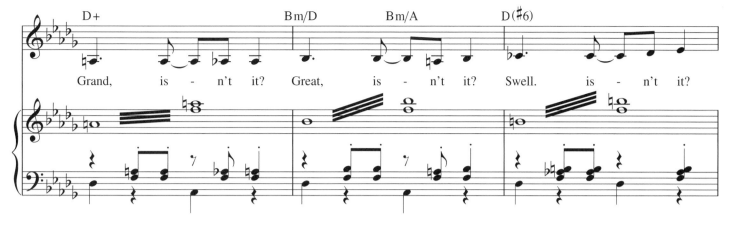

Grand, is - n't it? Great, is - n't it? Swell, is - n't it?

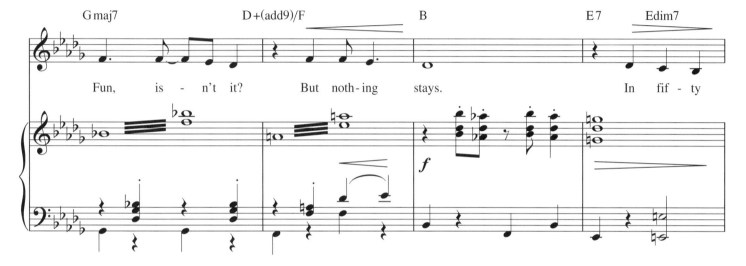

Fun, is - n't it? But noth-ing stays. In fif - ty

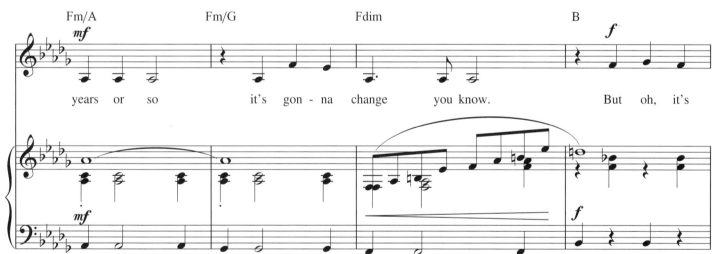

years or so it's gon-na change you know. But oh, it's

heav - en now - a - days.

On the Sunny Side of the Street

Lyric by DOROTHY FIELDS
Music by JIMMY McHUGH

Moderato

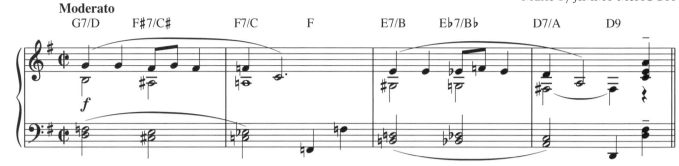

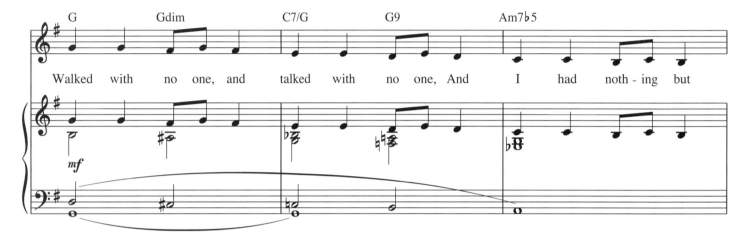

Walked with no one, and talked with no one, And I had noth-ing but

shad - ows   Then one morn-ing you passed

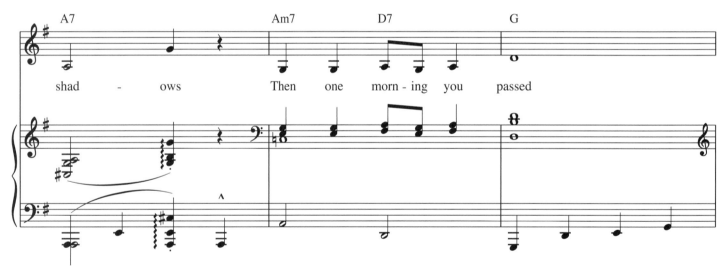

And I bright-ened at last   Now I greet the day,   and com-plete the day

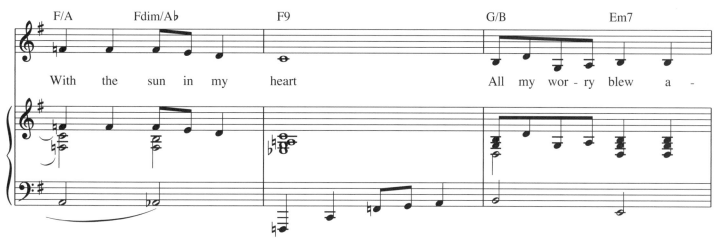

With the sun in my heart All my wor-ry blew a-

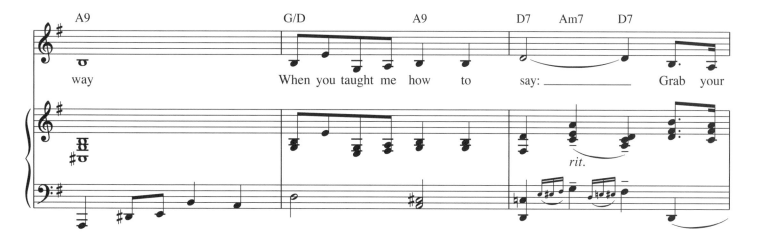

way When you taught me how to say: _____ Grab your

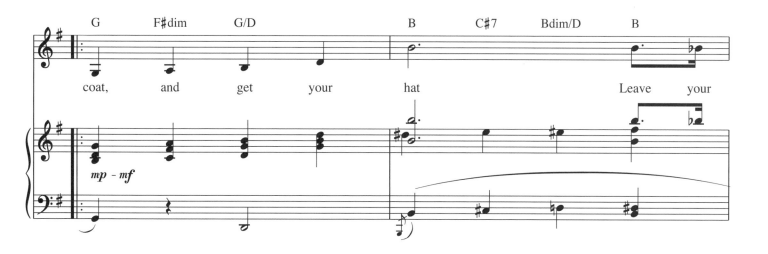

coat, and get your hat Leave your

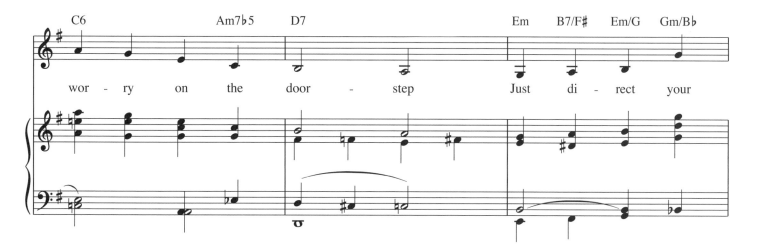

wor-ry on the door-step Just di-rect your

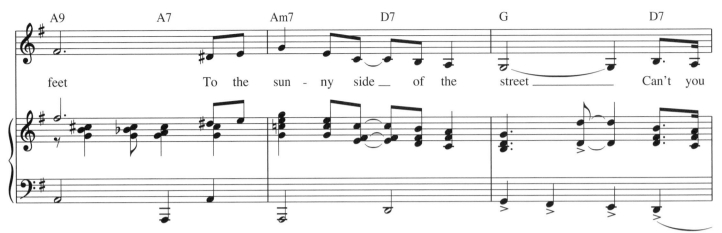

feet   To the sun - ny side __ of the   street _____   Can't you

hear   a   pit - ter - pat?   And   that   hap - py   tune   is

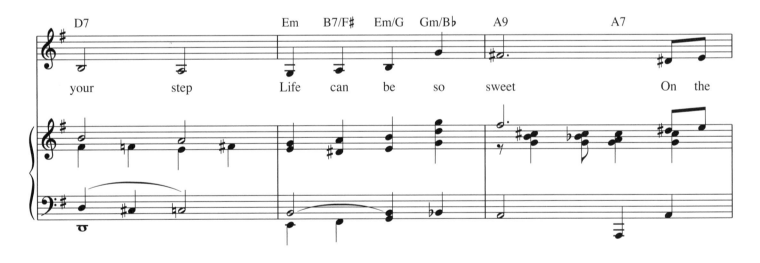

your   step   Life   can   be   so   sweet   On   the

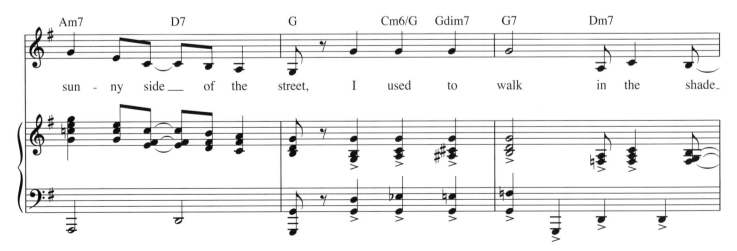

sun - ny side __ of the   street,   I   used   to   walk   in   the   shade __

With those blues on par - ade ___ But I'm not a - fraid ___

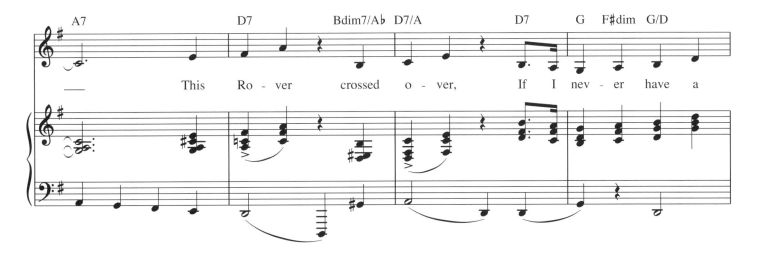

This Ro - ver crossed o - ver, If I nev - er have a

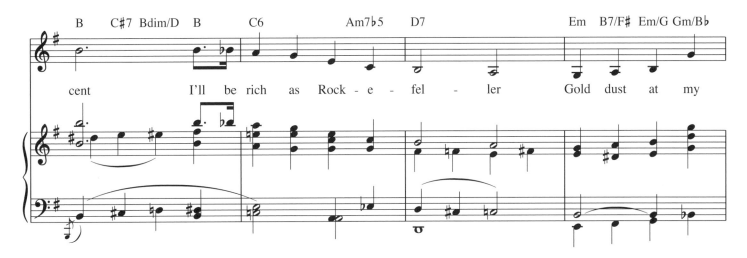

cent I'll be rich as Rock - e - fel - ler Gold dust at my

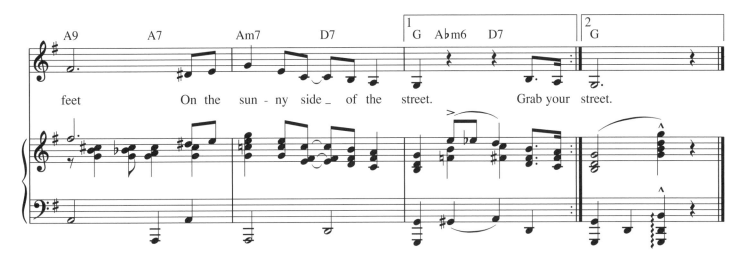

feet On the sun - ny side ___ of the street. Grab your street.

One for My Baby
(And One More for the Road)
from the Motion Picture THE SKY'S THE LIMIT

Lyric by JOHNNY MERCER
Music by HAROLD ARLEN

Lazily

It's quar-ter to three, __ there's no one in the place ex-

cept you and me, _____ so, set 'em up, Joe, __ I've

got a lit-tle sto - ry you ought-a know. _____ We're

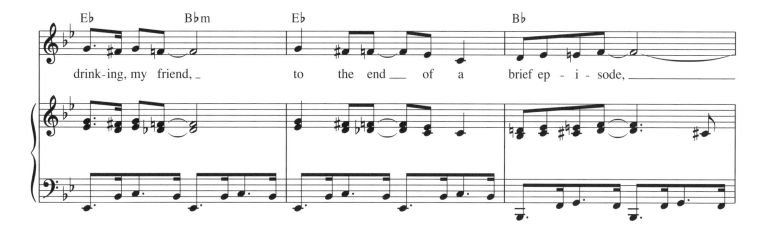

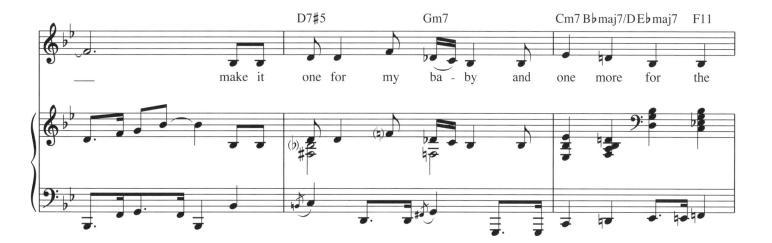

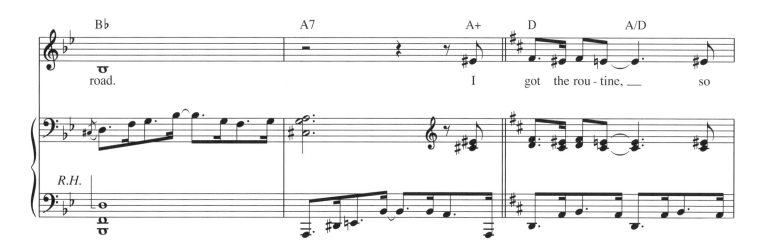

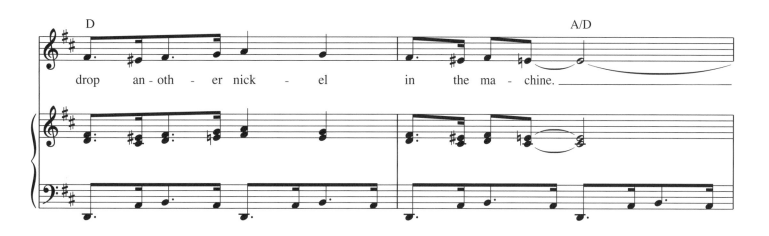

I'm feel-in' so bad,__ I wish you'd make the mu - sic dream-y and sad.__

Could tell you a lot, ___ but you've got ___ to be

true to your code,_____ make it one for my ba - by and

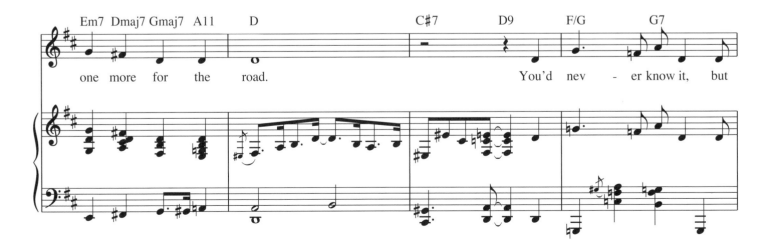

one more for the road. You'd nev - er know it, but

bud-dy, I'm a kind of po - et and I've got-ta lot - ta things to say._____ And

when I'm gloom-y, you sim-ply got-ta lis-ten to me, un - til it's talked a - way._____ Well,

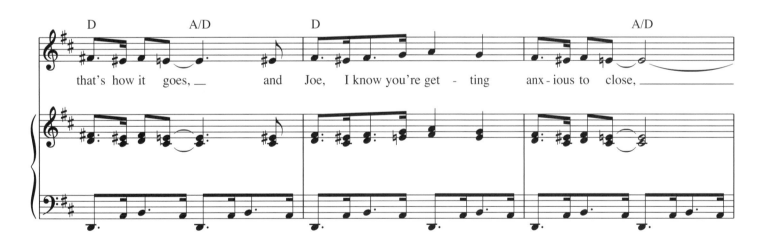

that's how it goes, __ and Joe, I know you're get - ting anx - ious to close, _____

_____ so, thanks for the cheer, __ I hope you did - n't mind my

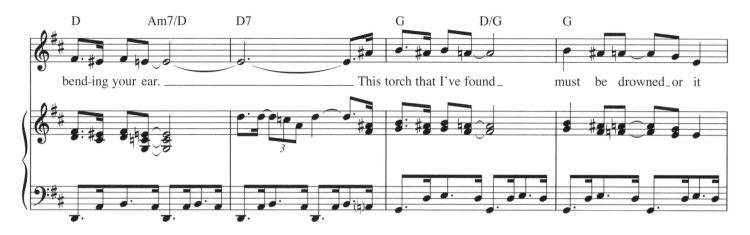

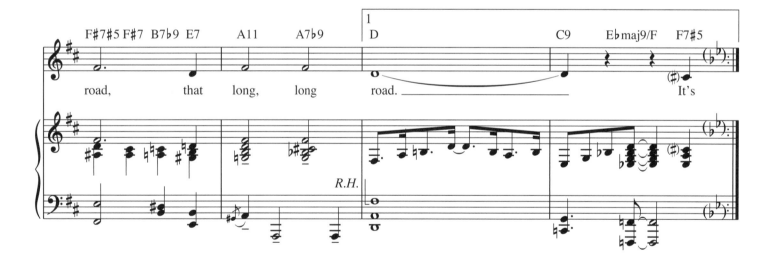

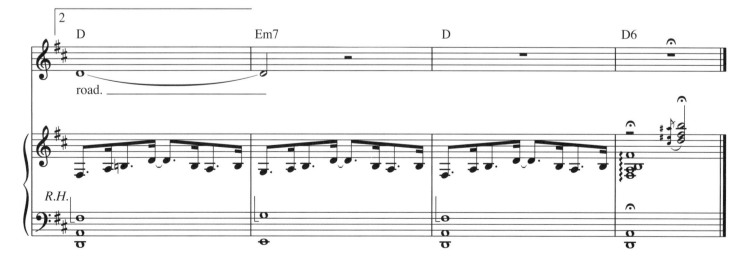

Sentimental Journey

Words and Music by BUD GREEN,
LES BROWN and BEN HOMER

got my res - er - va - tion, Spent each dime I could af - ford.

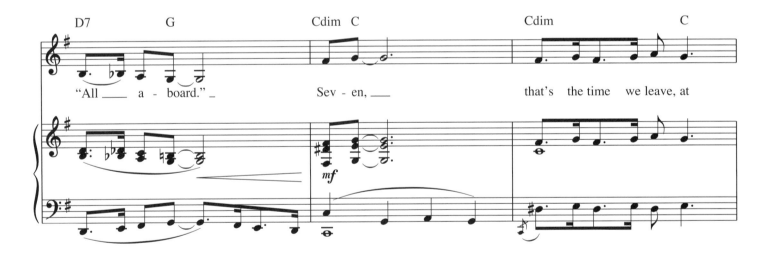

Like a child in wild an - ti - ci - pa - tion, Long to hear that

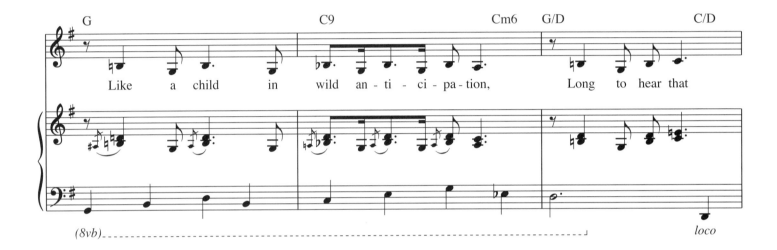

"All ___ a - board." ___ Sev - en, ___ that's the time we leave, at

sev - en. ___ I'll be wait - in' up for Heav - en, ___

Que Sera, Sera
(Whatever Will Be, Will Be)
from THE MAN WHO KNEW TOO MUCH

Words and Music by JAY LIVINGSTON
and RAY EVANS

Will I be rich?" Here's what she said to
Should I sing songs?" This was her wise re-

me: "Que se - ra, se - ra, _____ What-
ply:

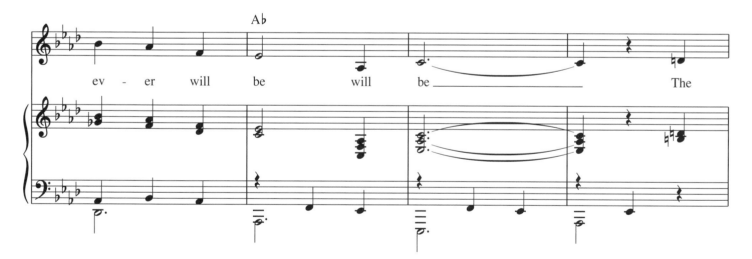

ev - er will be will be _____ The

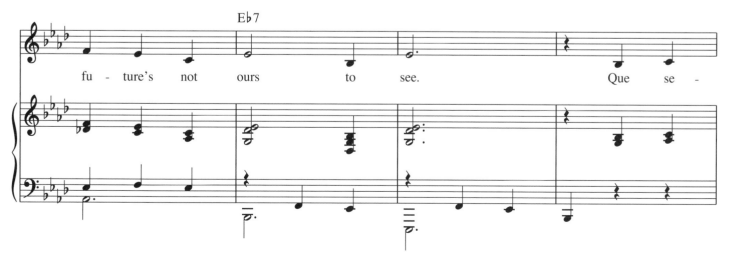

fu - ture's not ours to see. Que se -

ra, se - ra! _____ What will be will

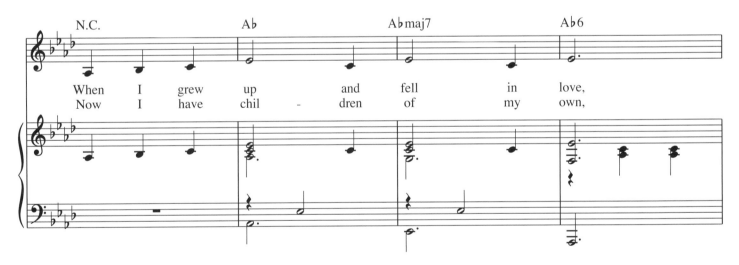

be!" _____ When I was _____

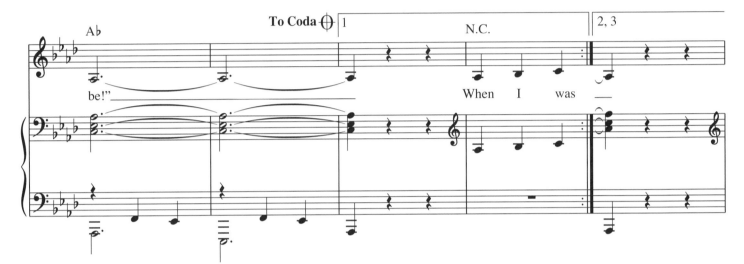

When I grew up and fell in love,
Now I have chil - dren of my own,

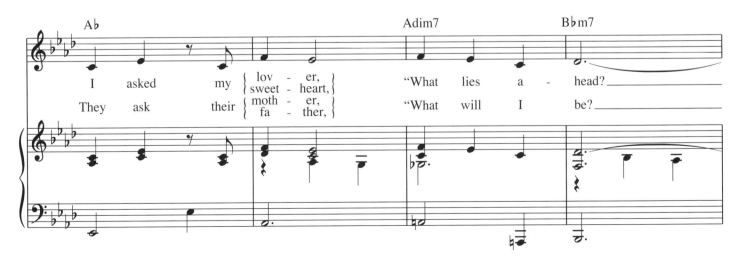

I asked my { lov - er, / sweet - heart, } "What lies a - head? _____
They ask their { moth - er, / fa - ther, } "What will I be? _____

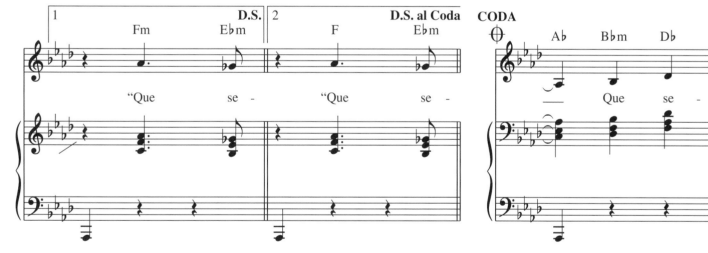

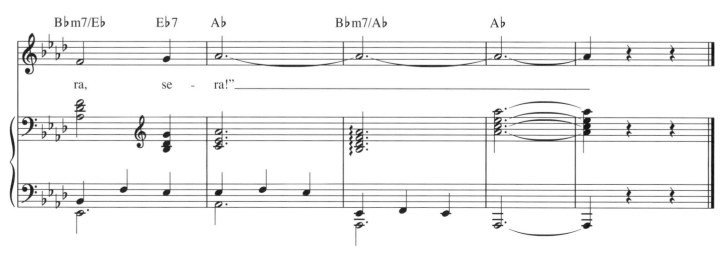

Stormy Weather
(Keeps Rainin' All the Time)
from COTTON CLUB PARADE OF 1933

Lyric by TED KOEHLER
Music by HAROLD ARLEN

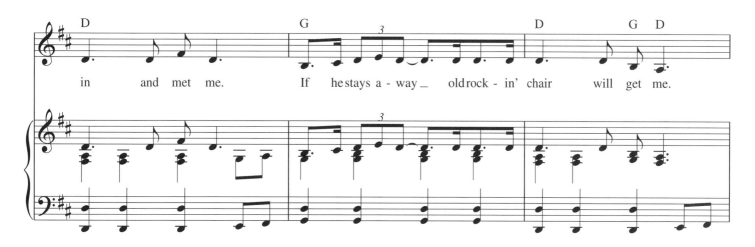

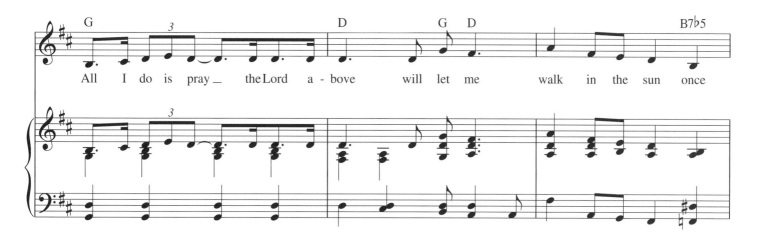

more. Can't go on, _____ ev - 'ry - thing I had is gone, Storm - y

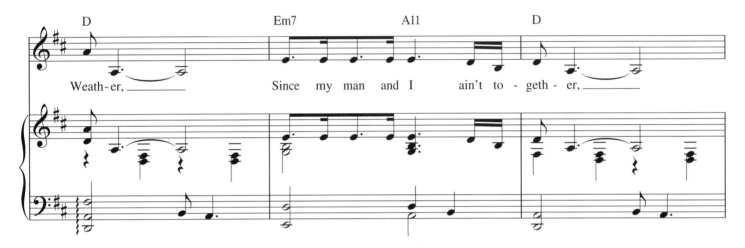

Weath-er, _____ Since my man and I ain't to - geth - er, _____

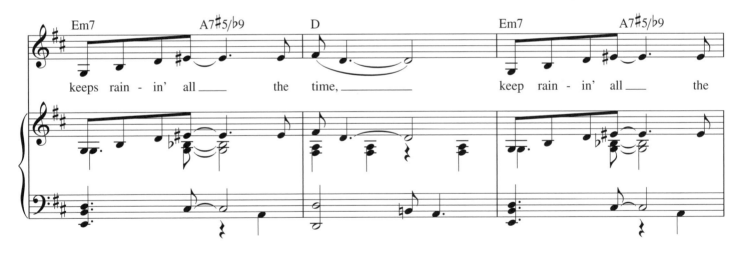

keeps rain - in' all ____ the time, _____ keep rain - in' all ____ the

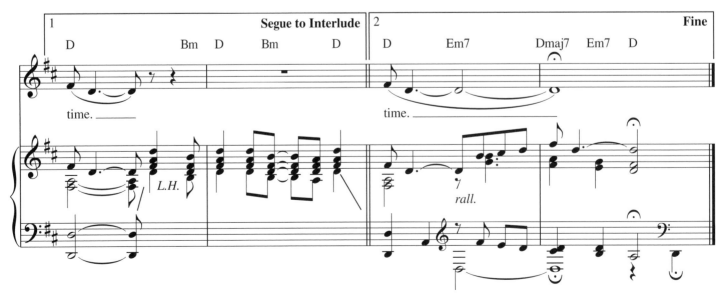

time. _____ time. _____

Interlude

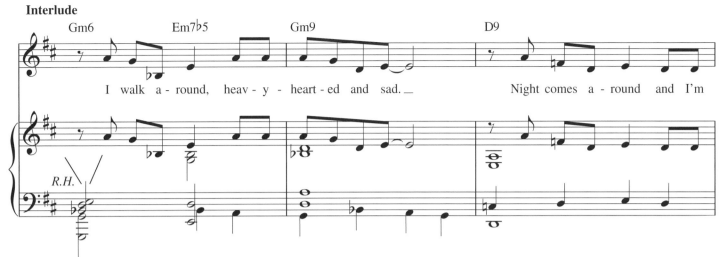

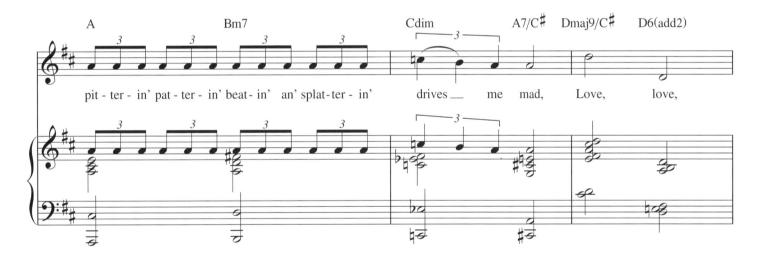

Ten Cents a Dance

from SIMPLE SIMON

Words by LORENZ HART
Music by RICHARD RODGERS

In moderate tempo

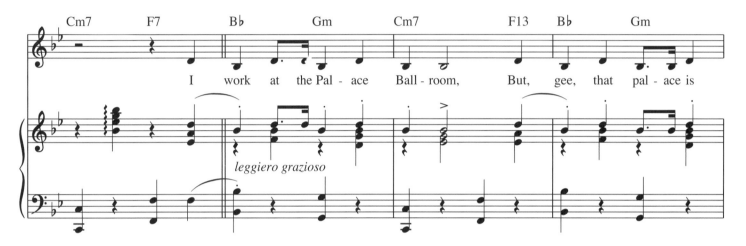

I work at the Pal-ace Ball-room, But, gee, that pal-ace is

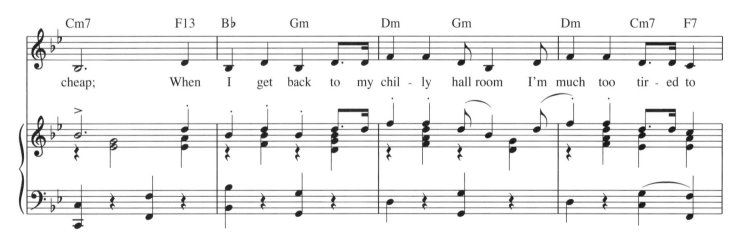

cheap; When I get back to my chil-ly hall room I'm much too tir-ed to

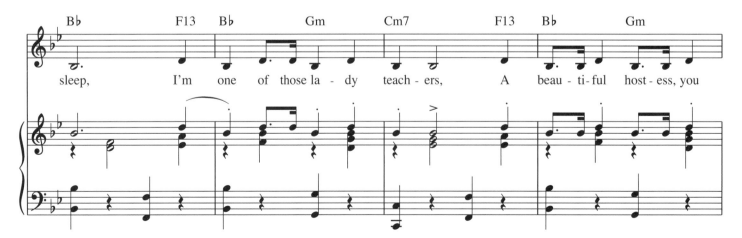

sleep, I'm one of those la-dy teach-ers, A beau-ti-ful host-ess, you

I'm here till clos-ing time, Dance and be mer-ry, it's
on-ly a dime. Some-times I think I've found my he - ro
But it's a queer ro - mance, All that you need __ is a
tick - et! Come on, big boy, ten cents a dance! __

Tenderly

from TORCH SONG

Lyric by JACK LAWRENCE
Music by WALTER GROSS

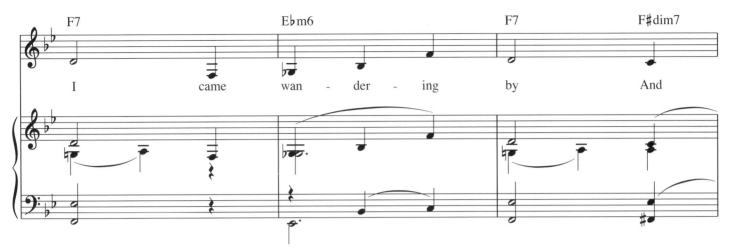

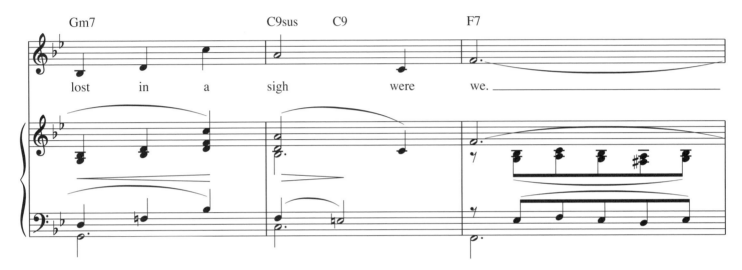

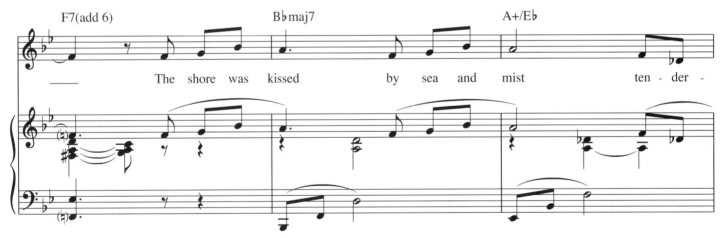

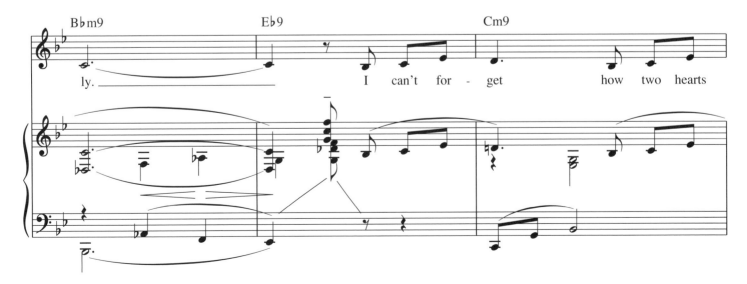

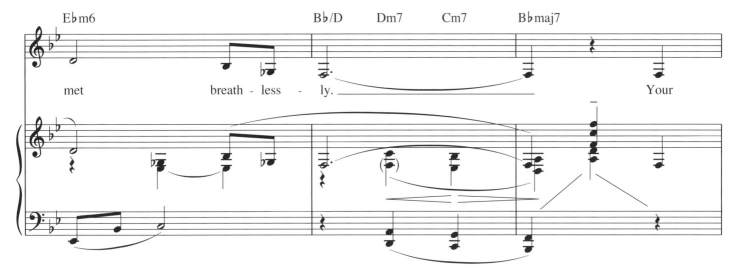

met breath - less - ly. _____ Your

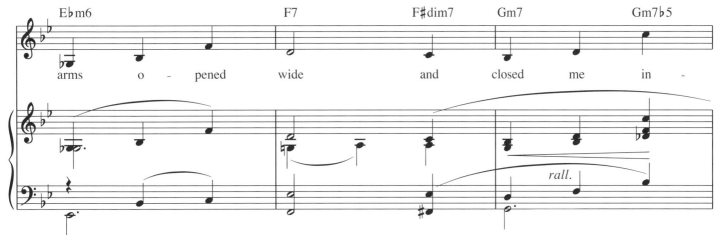

arms o - pened wide and closed me in -

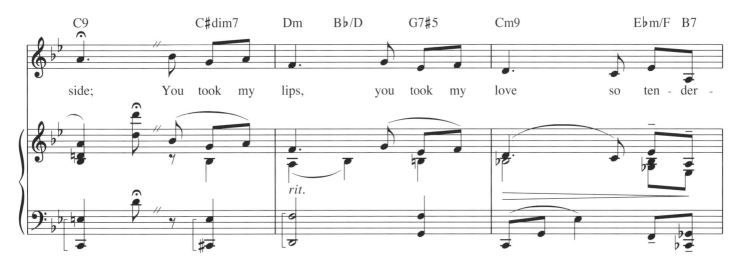

side; You took my lips, you took my love so ten - der -

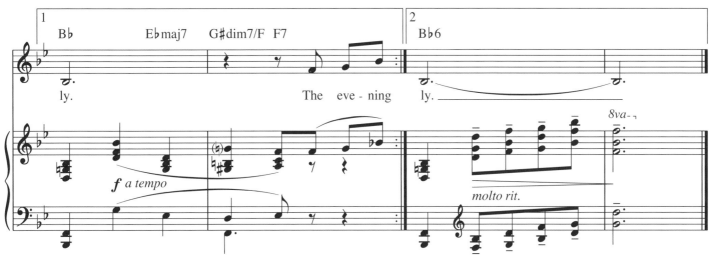

ly. The eve - ning ly. _____

That Old Black Magic

from the Paramount Picture STAR SPANGLED RHYTHM

Words by JOHNNY MERCER
Music by HAROLD ARLEN

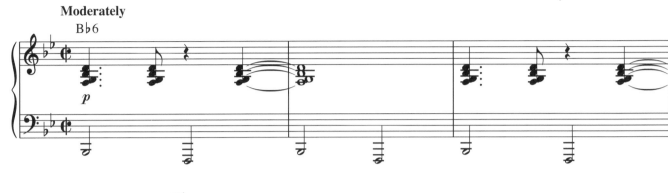

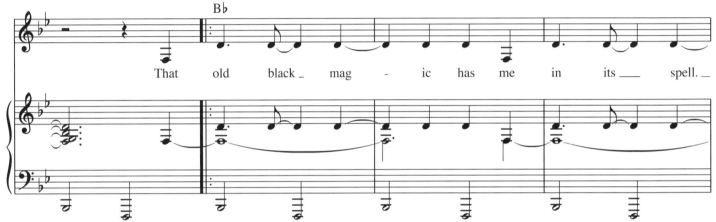

That old black mag - ic has me in its spell.

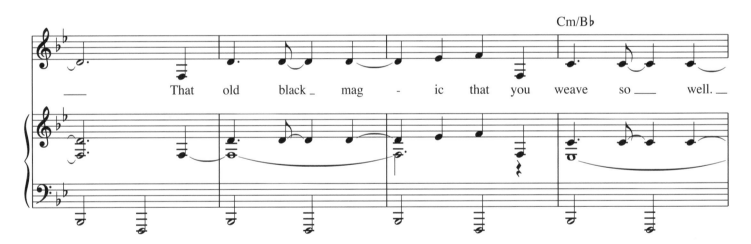

That old black mag - ic that you weave so well.

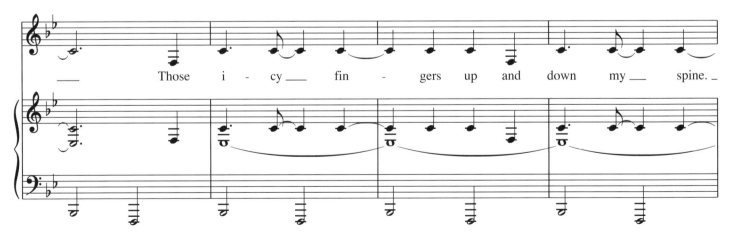

Those i - cy fin - gers up and down my spine.

The same old ___ witch - craft when your eyes meet ___ mine. ___

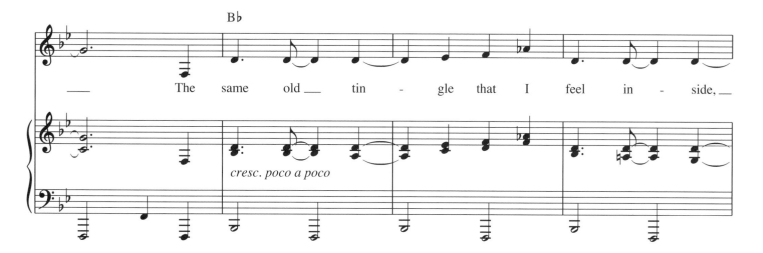

The same old ___ tin - gle that I feel in - side, ___

cresc. poco a poco

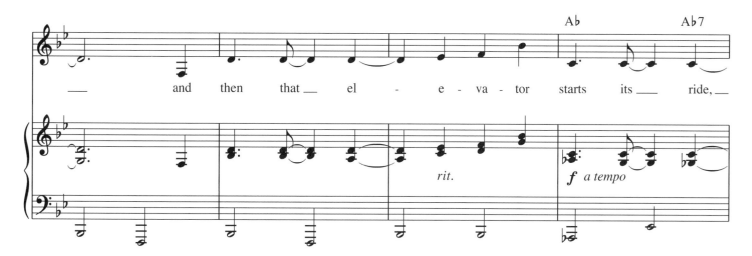

and then that ___ el - e - va - tor starts its ___ ride, ___

rit.   *ff a tempo*

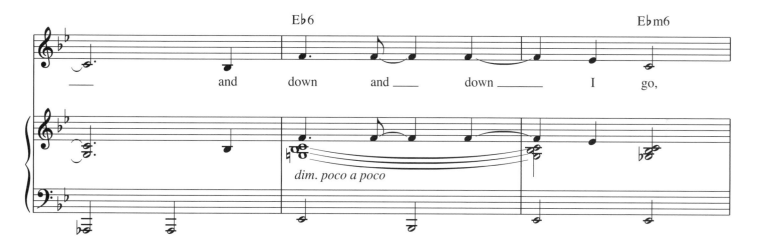

and down and ___ down _____ I go,

dim. poco a poco

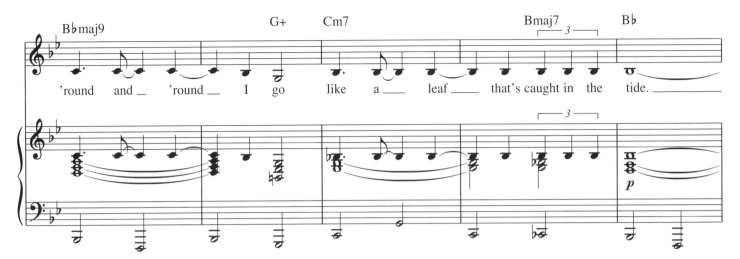

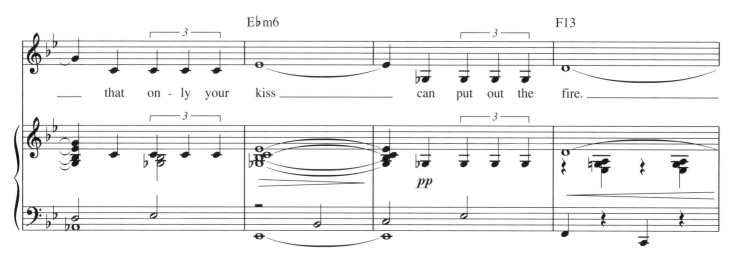

that on-ly your kiss ___ can put out the fire. ___

For you're the ___ lov - er I have wait - ed ___ for, ___

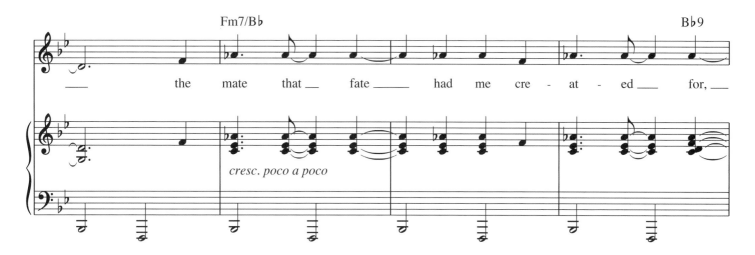

the mate that ___ fate ___ had me cre - at - ed ___ for, ___

and ev - 'ry ___ time ___ your lips meet mine, ___ dar - ling,

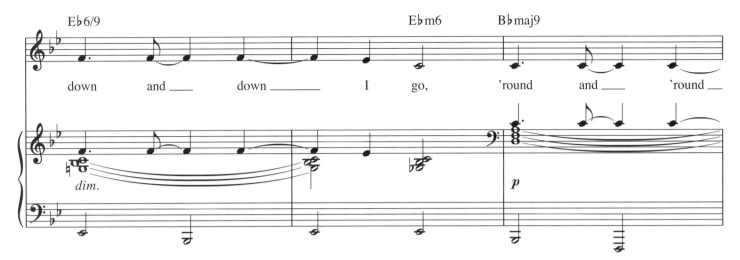

down and ___ down ___ I go, 'round and ___ 'round ___

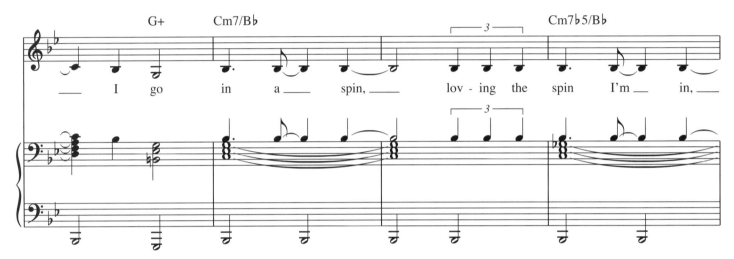

___ I go in a ___ spin, ___ lov-ing the spin I'm ___ in, ___

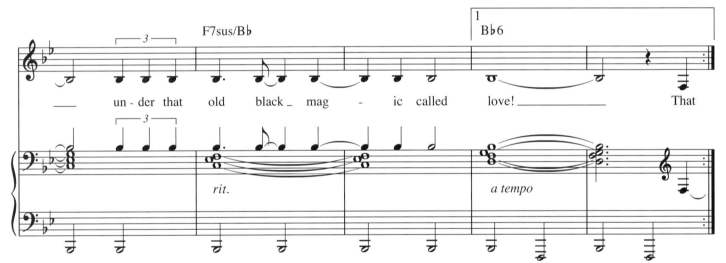

___ un-der that old black ___ mag - ic called love! _____ That

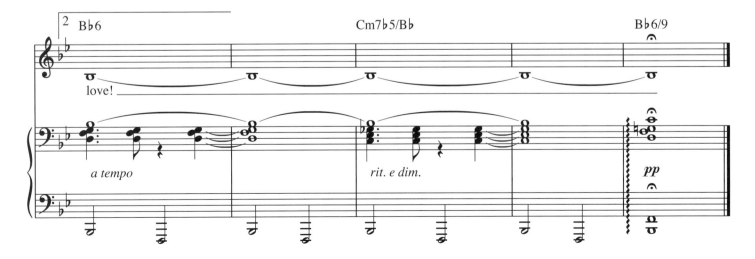

love! _____

When the Sun Comes Out

Lyric by TED KOEHLER
Music by HAROLD ARLEN

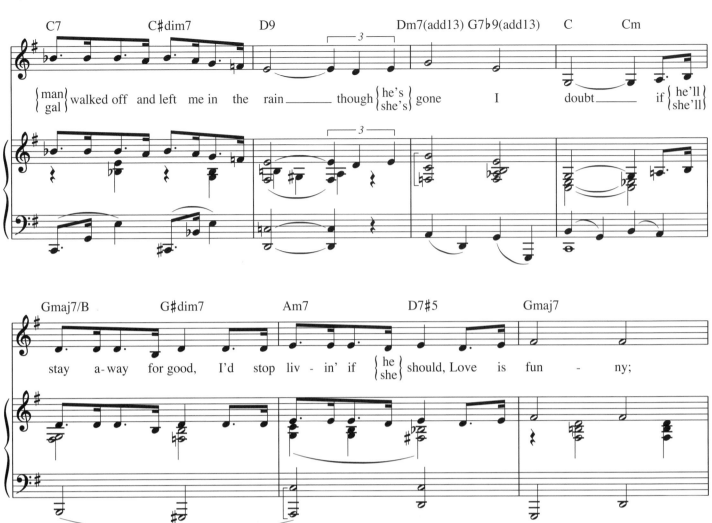

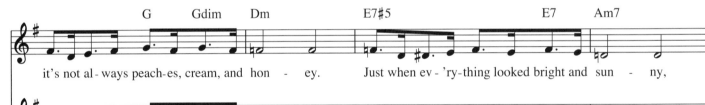

When I Fall in Love

Words by EDWARD HEYMAN
Music by VICTOR YOUNG

Slowly, with much feeling

When I fall in love it will be for-ev-er, or I'll nev-er

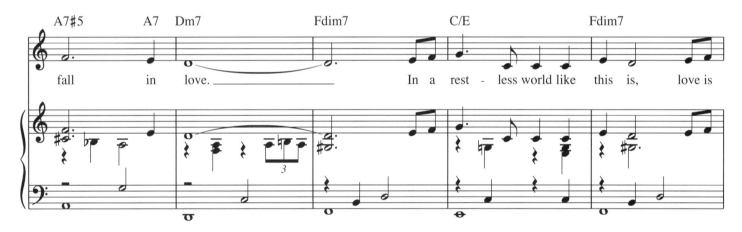

fall in love. _____ In a rest-less world like this is, love is

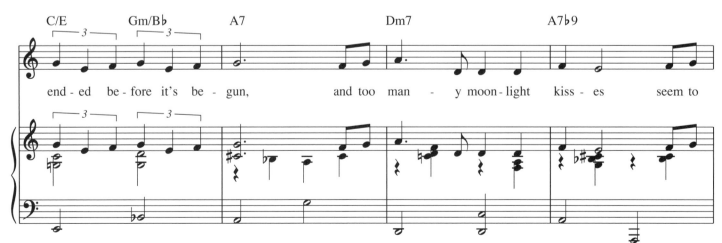

end-ed be-fore it's be-gun, and too man-y moon-light kiss-es seem to

Where or When

from BABES IN ARMS

Words by LORENZ HART
Music by RICHARD RODGERS

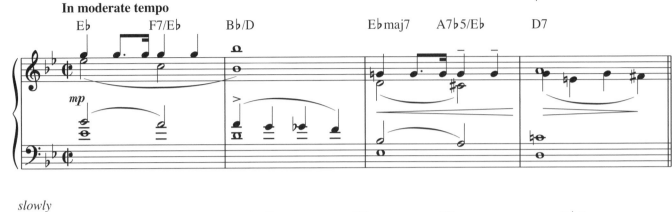

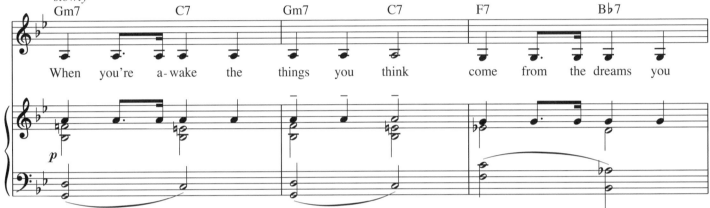

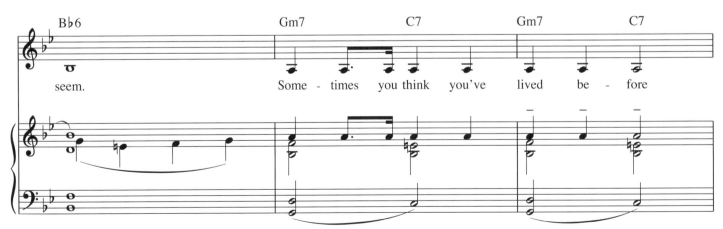

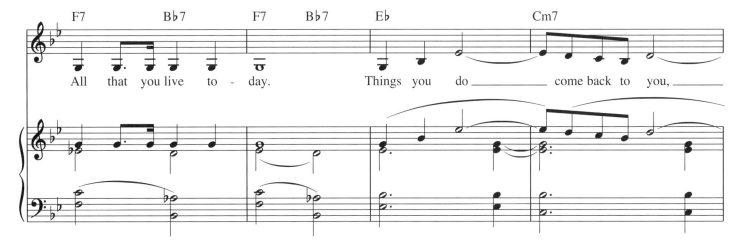

All that you live to - day. Things you do _____ come back to you, _____

_____ As though they knew the way. Oh, the tricks your mind can play!

poco rit.

(slowly, with very much sentiment)

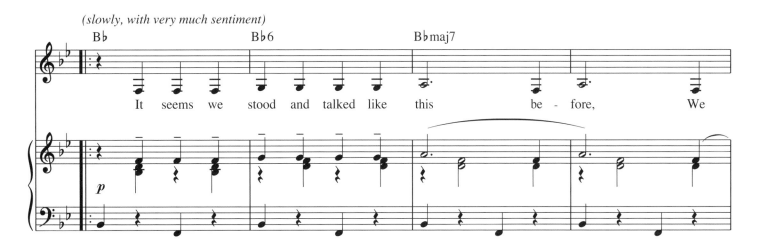

It seems we stood and talked like this be - fore, We

looked at each oth - er in the same way then, But I can't re-mem - ber where or

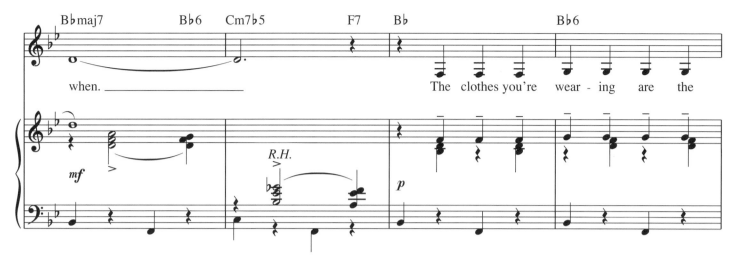

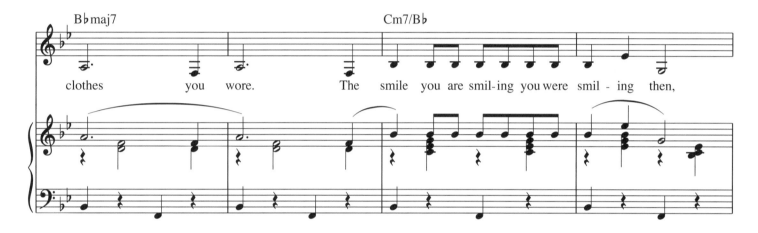

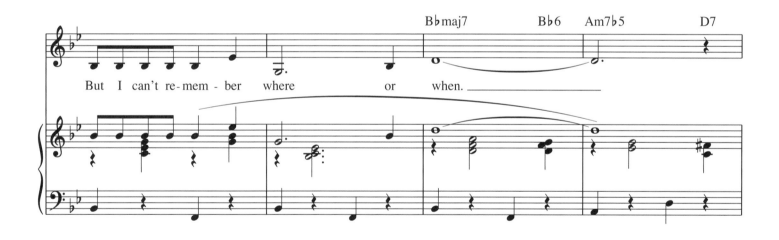

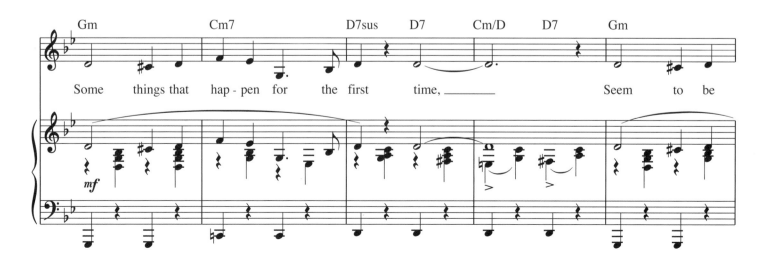

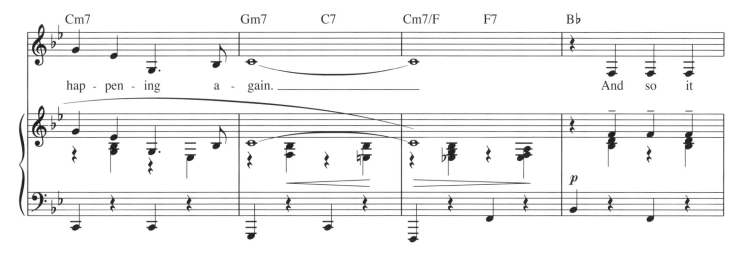

hap - pen - ing a - gain. _____ And so it

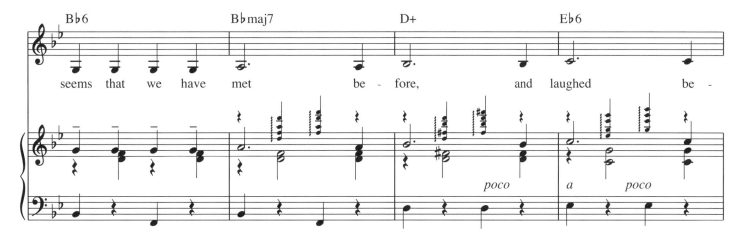

seems that we have met be - fore, and laughed be -

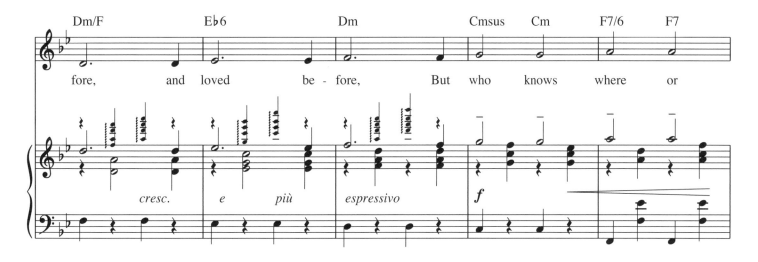

fore, and loved be - fore, But who knows where or

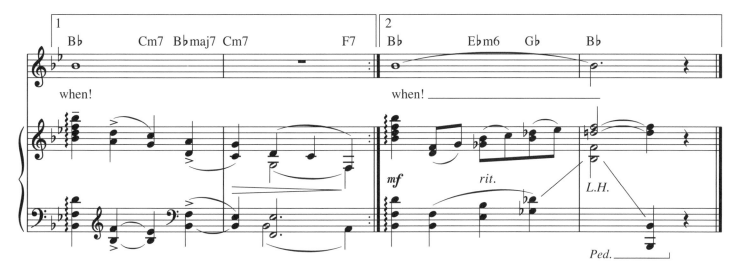

when! when! _____

Why Don't You Do Right

(Get Me Some Money, Too!)

By JOE McCOY

Slow blues tempo

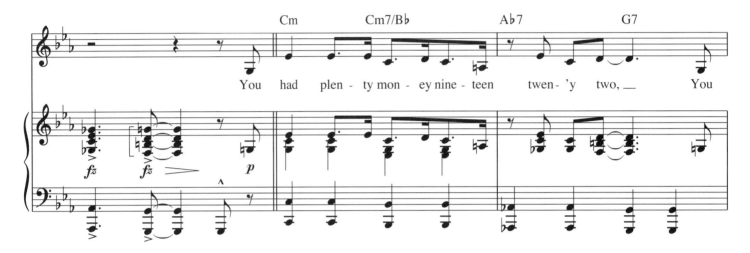

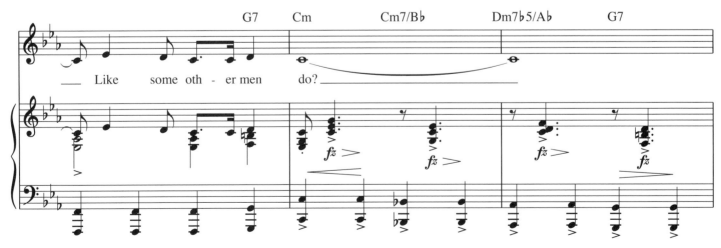

Get out of here and get me some mon-ey, too.

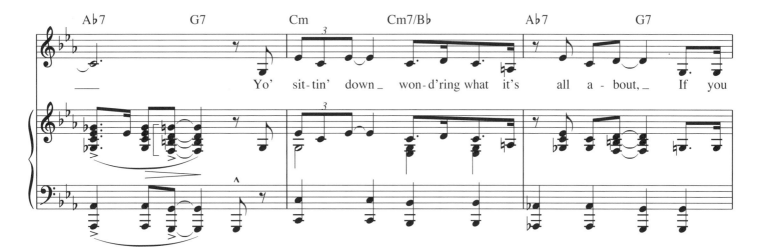

Yo' sit-tin' down won-d'ring what it's all a-bout, If you

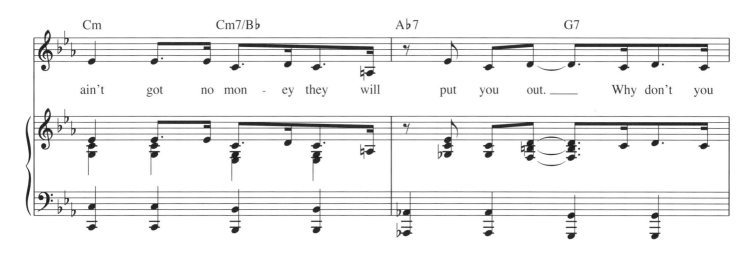

ain't got no mon-ey they will put you out. Why don't you

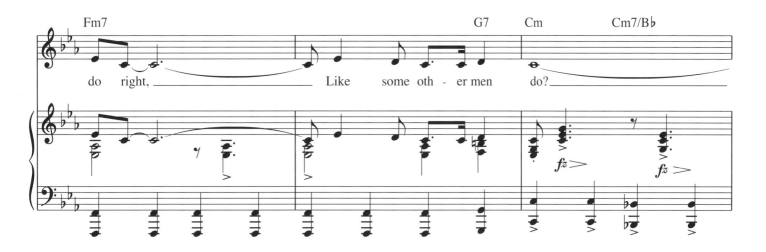

do right, Like some oth-er men do?

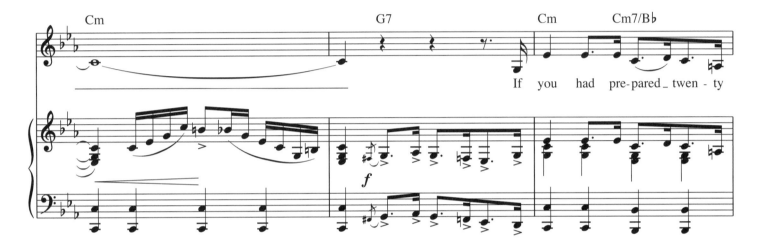

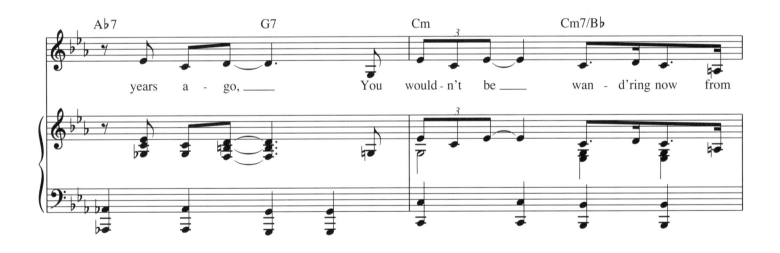

Why Was I Born?

from SWEET ADELINE

Lyrics by OSCAR HAMMERSTEIN II
Music by JEROME KERN

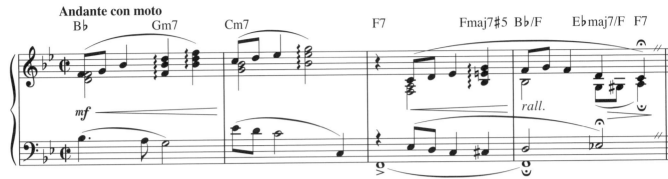

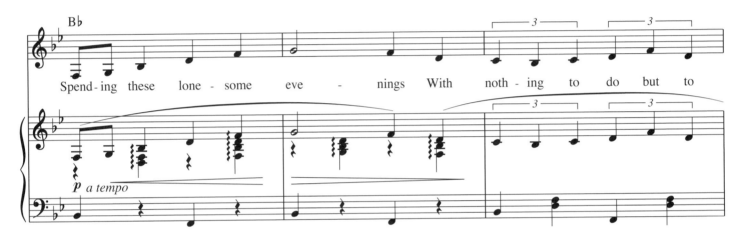

Spend-ing these lone-some eve - nings With noth-ing to do but to

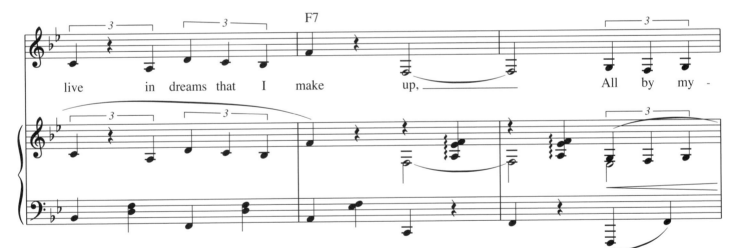

live in dreams that I make up, All by my -

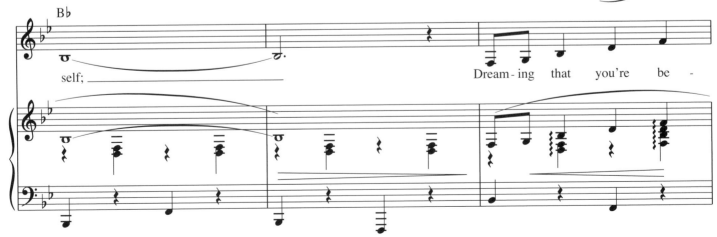

self; Dream-ing that you're be -

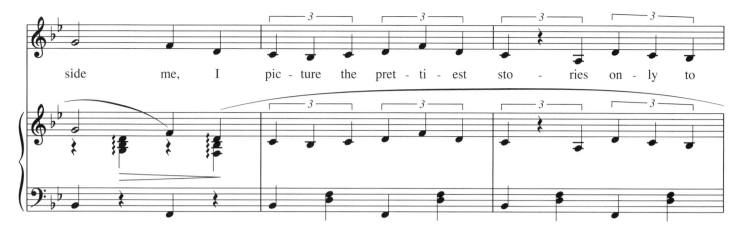

side me, I pic - ture the pret - ti - est sto - ries on - ly to

wake up, _____ All by my - self. _____

What is the good of me, by my - self? _____

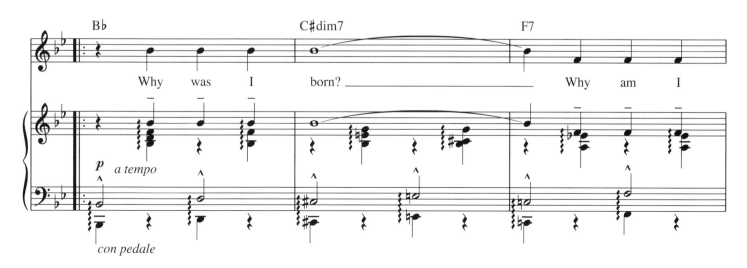

Why was I born? _____ Why am I

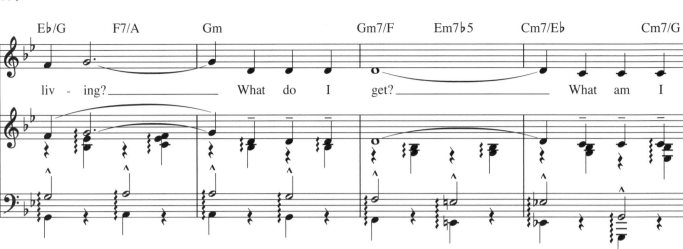

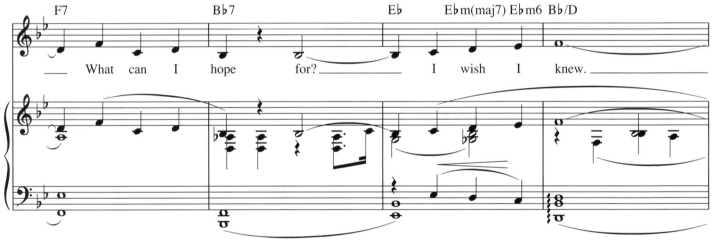

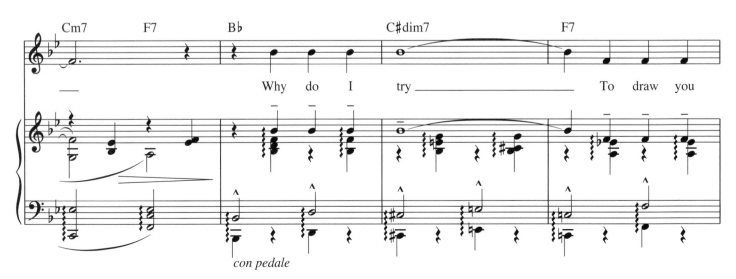

You Brought a New Kind of Love to Me

from the Paramount Picture THE BIG POND

Words and Music by SAMMY FAIN,
IRVING KAHAL and PIERRE NORMAN

than they do ___ For you've brought a new kind of love to me.

If the sand-man brought ___ me dreams of you ___ I'd want to sleep my

whole life thru, ___ For you've brought a new kind of love to me. ___

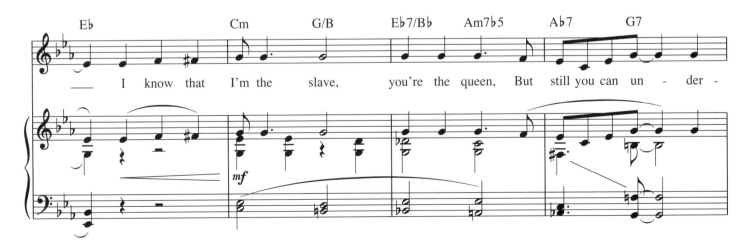

___ I know that I'm the slave, you're the queen, But still you can un - der -

You Took Advantage of Me

from PRESENT ARMS

Words by LORENZ HART
Music by RICHARD RODGERS

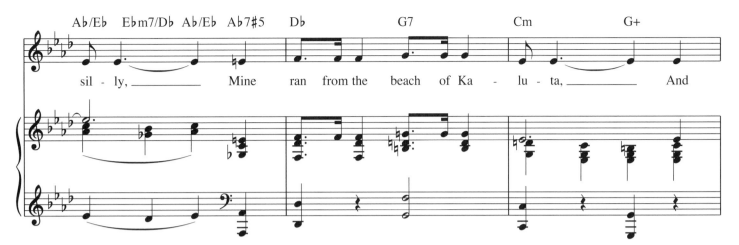

sil - ly, _____ Mine ran from the beach of Ka - lu - ta, _____ And

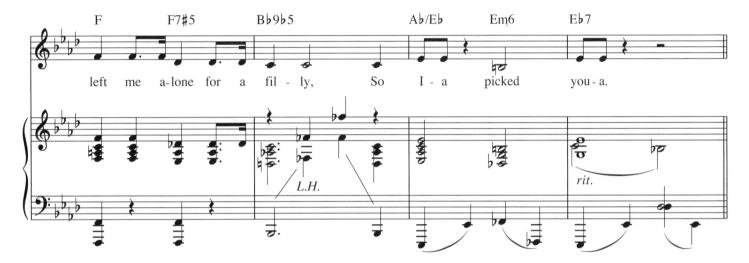

left me a-lone for a fil - ly, So I - a picked you - a.

(liltingly)

I'm a sen - ti-men - tal sap, that's all. __ What's the use of try - ing

not to fall? __ I have no will, __ You've made your kill __ 'Cause you

took ad - van - tage of me! I'm just like an ap - ple

on a bough __ And you're gon - na shake me down some - how, __ So

what's the use, __ you've cooked my goose __ 'Cause you took ad - van - tage of me!

I'm so hot and both - ered that I don't know __ My el - bow from __ my

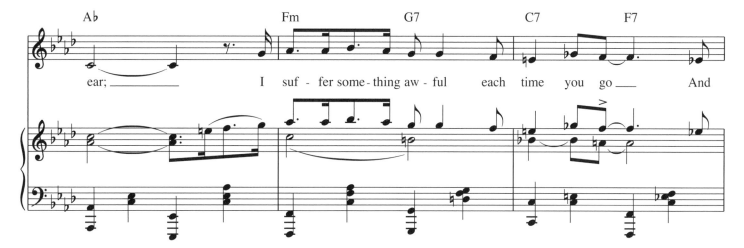

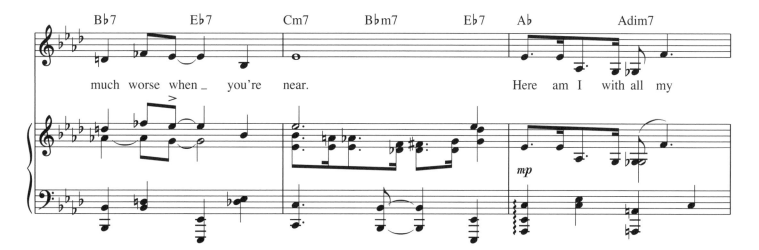

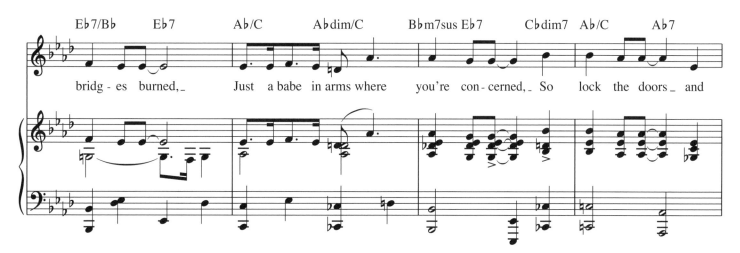

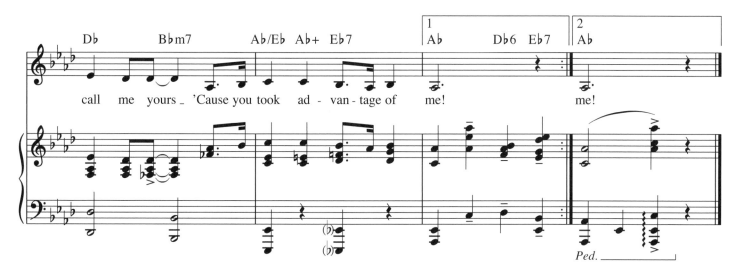

Why Did I Choose You?

from THE YEARLING

Lyric by HERBERT MARTIN
Music by MICHAEL LEONARD

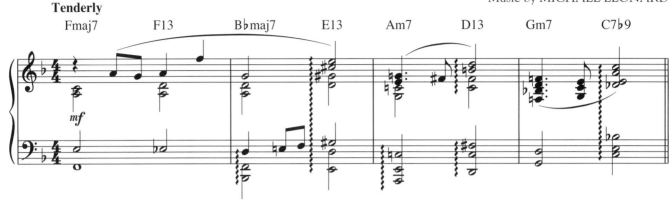

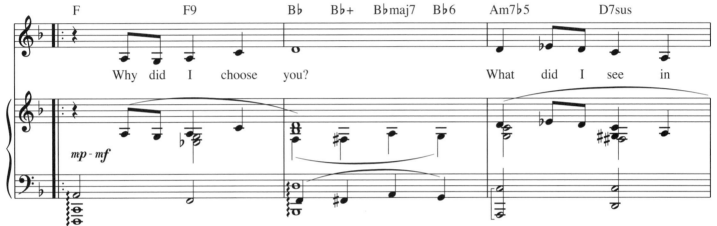

Why did I choose you? What did I see in you?

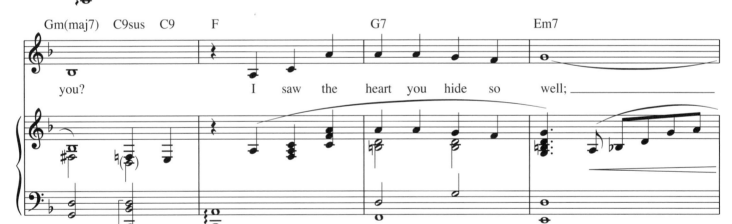

you? I saw the heart you hide so well;

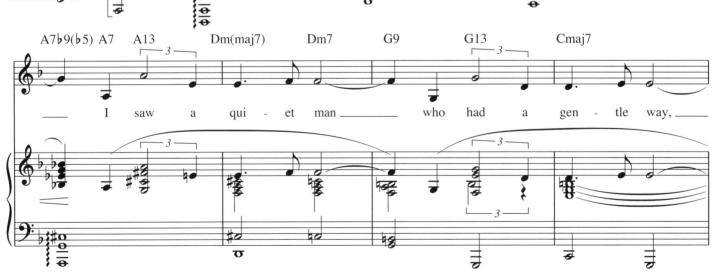

I saw a qui-et man who had a gen-tle way,

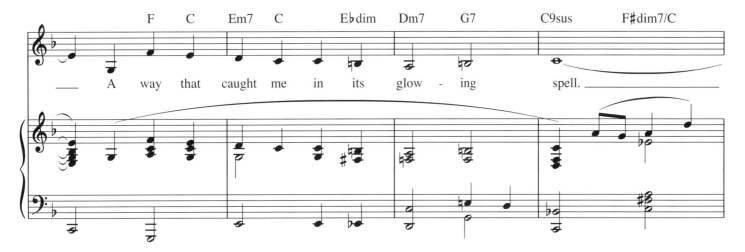

A way that caught me in its glow - ing spell.

Why did I want your, What could you of - fer

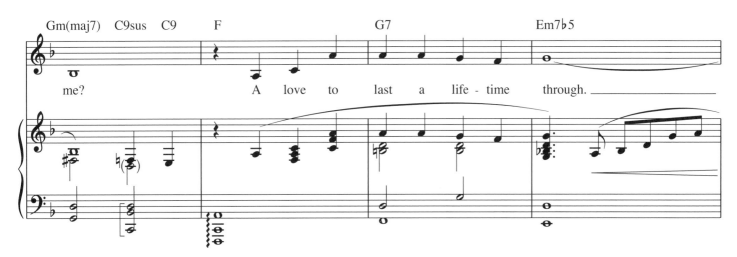

me? A love to last a life - time through.

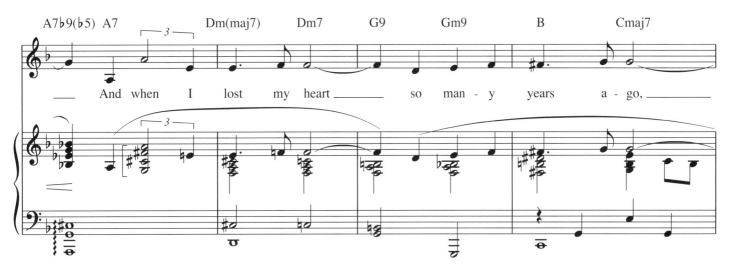

And when I lost my heart so man - y years a - go,

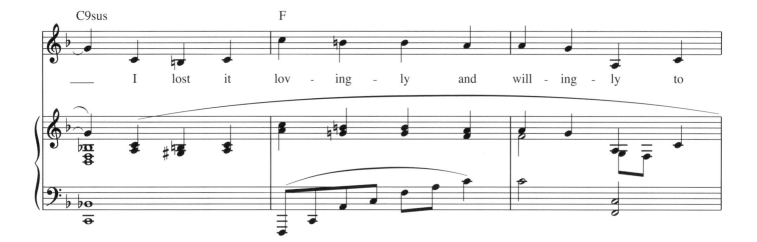

I lost it lov - ing - ly and will - ing - ly to

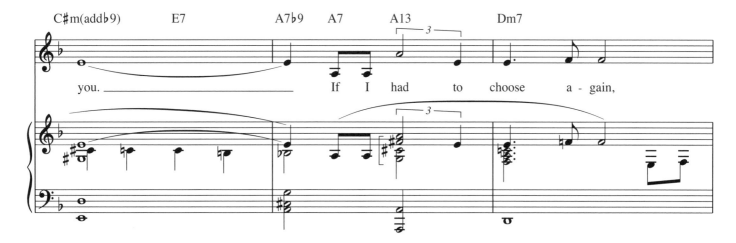

you. _____ If I had to choose a - gain,

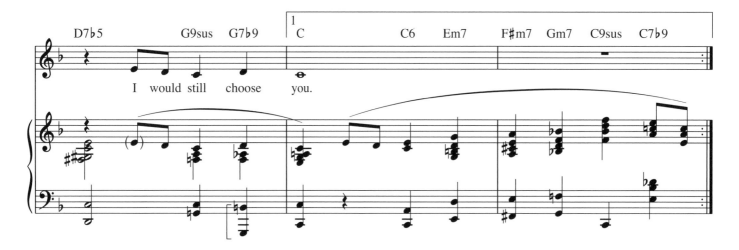

I would still choose you.

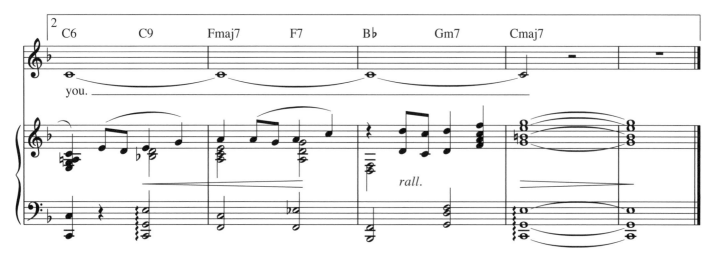

you. _____